CULTURES OF THE WORLD

FIJI

Roseline NgCheong-Lum

MARSHALL CAVENDISH
New York • London • Sydney

Reference edition reprinted 2005 by
Marshall Cavendish Corporation
99 White Plains Road
Tarrytown, NY 10591
Website: www.marshallcavendish.us

© Times Media Private Limited 2000
© Marshall Cavendish International (Asia) Private Limited 2005

Originated and designed by Times Books International
An imprint of Marshall Cavendish International (Asia) Private Limited
A member of the Times Publishing Group

Library of Congress Cataloging-in-Publication Data
NgCheong-Lum, Roseline, 1962–
Fiji / Roseline NgCheong-Lum.
   p. cm. — (Cultures of the world)
Includes bibliographical references and index.
Summary: Describes the geography, history, government, economy, people, lifestyle,
religion, language, arts, leisure, festivals, and food of South Pacific island of Fiji.
ISBN 0-7614-0996-3 (lib. bdg.)
1. Fiji—Juvenile literature. [1. Fiji.] I. Title. II. Series.
DU600.N45   2001
996.11—dc21   99-054120
                              CIP
                              AC

Printed in Malaysia

INTRODUCTION

Called the "Gateway to the South Pacific," Fiji is a crossroads of cultures. This archipelago consists of more than 300 volcanic islands and low-lying atolls. White sandy beaches, impenetrable rainforests, shifting sand dunes, and reefs teeming with marine life all form part of Fiji's landscape.

Once feared for their reputation as fierce cannibals, Fiji Islanders are today one of the most friendly people on earth. The population consists of Fijians, Indians, Polynesians, Chinese, and Europeans, who live side by side as separate entities. While calling Fiji their home, the migrant communities have retained their ancestral religions, customs, and cultures. In the course of a tumultuous history, the nonindigenous Fiji Islanders have suffered grave injustices. But with the declaration of a new nondiscriminatory constitution, Fiji has been accepted back into the world community, and all Fiji Islanders are looking forward to economic and social progress.

CONTENTS

A Fijian man on his way to the market to sell his produce.

CONTENTS

Blue skies and a peaceful landscape form a typical picture of a summer afternoon in Fiji.

GEOGRAPHY

SPRAWLING OVER AN AREA of about 501,800 square miles (1,300,000 square km) in the fabled South Seas, the Fijian archipelago is made up of about 330 islands, of which about one-third are inhabited. Lying just north of the Tropic of Capricorn, the country is slightly larger than California and Nevada put together. Less than 1.5% of the territory is land; the rest is sea. The 180° meridian, the International Date Line that divides the world into today (on the west side) and yesterday (on the east side), passes through the islands. Fiji is the dividing point between Melanesia and Polynesia. To the east are the low coral atolls of Polynesia. Moving west, these atolls give way to the mountainous volcanic islands of Melanesia.

The nearest large city is Auckland in New Zealand, which is located about 1,300 miles (2,092 km) to the south. Honolulu is only five hours away by air, while Los Angeles is a ten-hour flight.

Left: **There are so many islands in Fiji that it is often possible to have a whole stretch of sand and sea to yourself.**

Opposite: **Waya Island, situated in the Yasawa Group, has many rugged hills and beautiful beaches and lagoons.**

THE FIJIAN ARCHIPELAGO

Fiji is composed of two large islands, Viti Levu and Vanua Levu, rimmed by groups of islands on both sides. The whole archipelago surrounds the Koro Sea.

The largest island is Viti Levu. Meaning "Big Fiji," it is the third largest of all the islands in the Pacific and is the hub of the Fijian archipelago. The most developed island in the archipelago, Viti Levu is home to 70% of the Fijian population. One peculiarity of this island is the large contrast between east and west. While the eastern side is very wet and green, the western part is dry and sun-baked. It is the western coast that most tourists visit, and where large areas of sugarcane plantations are located.

The Nadi International Airport is the main airport in Fiji.

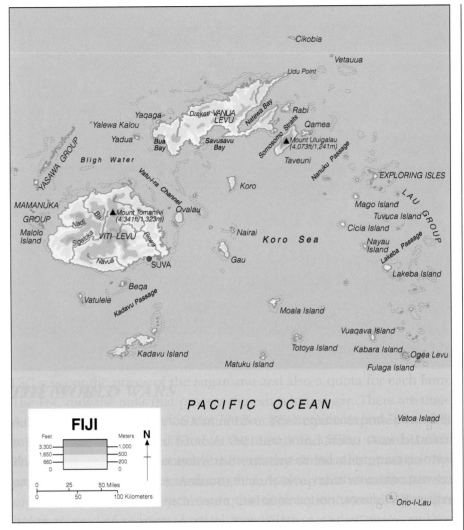

FIJI

Feet		Meters	N ↑
3,300		1,000	
1,650		500	
660		200	
0		0	

0	25	50 Miles
0	50	100 Kilometers

Kadavu is the first landmark for visitors arriving from the south and is a good place for nature lovers.

Suva, the largest city, port, and capital of Fiji, is on the southeastern shore. The Nausori Highlands is a spectacular mountain region in the central part of the island. Viti Levu is home to the country's highest mountain, Mount Tomaniivi, and the longest river, Rewa River. Off the east coast of Viti Levu is a small island, Bau. The former native capital, Bau is the home of the high chiefs of Fiji. Kadavu, the third largest island in Fiji, is located 62 miles (100 km) south of Suva. Rotuma, a Polynesian island 440 miles (708 km) to the north of Suva, also belongs to Fiji. It has an area of 18 square miles (47 square km).

REEFS

Coral reefs have existed for thousands of years. Coral consists of polyps, which are soft living organisms, and a hard calcium carbonate secreted by the polyps. It takes billions of polyps thousands of years to produce a few square miles of reef. Coral reefs are home to over 25% of all marine life and are among the world's most fragile and endangered ecosystems. Many reefs around the world have been damaged

by human activity. If undisturbed, the coral continues to build on itself and grow in size. Millions of polyps live on top of the limestone remains of former colonies to create the massive reefs. The color and shape of the coral depend on a number of factors, including the amount of light the coral receives and the water quality.

The waters off Fiji are home to some of the most beautiful coral reefs in the world. In fact, Fiji has been called the "Soft Coral Capital of the World" by enthusiastic divers. There are three types of reefs in Fiji: "fringing" reefs along the coastline, "barrier" reefs separated from the coast by a lagoon, and "atoll" reefs, which are circular or horseshoe-shaped. The Great Astrolabe Reef, Rainbow Reef, Great Sea Reef, and the Argo Reef in the Lau Islands are among the most famous coral reefs in Fiji. The challenge for the Fijian government is to protect the precious reefs, while generating revenue from tourism and diving.

Vanua Levu, the second largest island, is about half the size of Viti Levu. Its name means "Big Land," and it is home to about 18% of the total population. Much less developed than its neighbor, the island is rugged and surrounded by an extensive system of coral reefs. Volcanic in origin, the island has few beaches. Wide geographical contrasts can be seen between the different regions. The interior is wild and mountainous, while the western district is arid and sunburned. The southern coast is cut by several wide bays fringed with palms. Vanua Levu used to be the center of the copra trade, but today sugar cultivation is the most important industry, and large cane fields can be seen on the dry western and northern coasts. Taveuni is a rather large island to the southeast of Vanua Levu. It is notable for Mount Uluigalau, which lies directly under the International Date Line, and the indigenous *tagimaucia* flower, which grows only here.

The Lau Group is made up of 57 islands to the east of Vanua Levu. Although scattered over more than 43,232 square miles (112,000 square km), their total land area is only 62 square miles (160 square km). The islands in the southern part of the group are closer to Tonga than to Suva, and they display quite a bit of Polynesian influence. Lakeba, a central island, is a meeting place between Fijians and Tongans, and serves as the traditional political center of the whole group.

Lomaiviti, or Central Fiji, consists of seven large volcanic islands and a few small ones east of Viti Levu. Ovalau is separated from Viti Levu by 10 miles (16 km) of shallow sea. Levuka, on Ovalau, was the capital of Fiji until 1882. Situated at the foot of a steep bluff, it has all the ambience of a 19th-century whaling town.

The Yasawa Group is a crescent-shaped chain of islands to the northwest of Viti Levu. There are 16 islands and numerous islets, all of volcanic origin. Since they are located on the leeside of Viti Levu, the islands are dry and sunny all year round. Although Turtle Island has a five-star hotel, the Yasawa Group is largely untouched by tourism.

Diving in the Great Astrolabe Reef. Located north of Kadavu, the Great Astrolabe Reef is the world's third largest fringing reef.

CLIMATE

Fiji enjoys a tropical maritime climate tempered by the southeast trade winds. The country experiences very slight temperature variations between the seasons. Summer lasts from October to March, with daytime highs of 85°F (29°C) and high levels of humidity. Winter temperatures average 68°F (20°C). In general, temperatures are cooler at higher elevations, especially in the mountainous interior of the large islands. Most rain falls in the summer months. The average annual rainfall is 120 inches (305 cm). The western parts of the Fiji Islands receive virtually no rain from April to October.

Hurricanes strike the archipelago on average once every two years. The months of November to April are dubbed the "hurricane season." Hurricanes develop from low-pressure centers near the equator. They usually reach their full force in latitudes such as Fiji's. Nevertheless very destructive hurricanes are rare in Fiji. From 1940 to 1980, only 12 out of 52 hurricanes were considered severe. In 1985 four cyclones hit Fiji within four months, causing extensive damage to agriculture and resulting in many deaths. The storms caused millions of dollars in damage to towns, agriculture, and the tourist industry.

PEAKS AND RIVERS

The larger islands are quite mountainous, rising abruptly from the shore to impressive heights. Most of them are of volcanic origin, as shown by the volumes of volcanic sediments and limstone deposits found. The highest peak in the country is Mount Tomaniivi on Viti Levu. Formerly called Mount Victoria, it rises to a height of 4,341 feet (1,323 m). Several other mountains tower at more than 3,000 feet (914 m).

Fiji also has many waterways. The longest river is the Rewa on Viti Levu, navigable for 81 miles (130 km) from its mouth. Other rivers on Viti Levu include the Sigatoka and Ba. Vanua Levu also has many rivers, although they are not as long as those on Viti Levu. The largest is the Dreketi.

Left: **A boatman navigating his raft to shore.**

Opposite: **Because it is surrounded by a vast expanse of sea, Fiji enjoys a stable tropical maritime climate throughout the year.**

FLORA

Almost half of Fiji's land area is still covered with rainforest. Forested areas are mainly found in the high plateau regions. Rainforest species include the *dakua* and *yaka*, which are durable woods used to make furniture. These species are becoming rarer, because new trees are not planted after excessive logging. There are several edible ferns in Fiji, known as *ota*. Another edible plant is the *nama* or grapeweed. Fijians consider it a delicacy.

Casuarina, pandanus, and coconut palms grow in the dry coastal areas. Fiji has several species of pandanus, which are grown around villages. The leaves can be used to thatch roofs and for making baskets and mats. Mangrove swamps also cover the eastern coastlines, while dry grasslands are found in the western areas of the large islands. More than 3,000 species

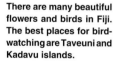

There are many beautiful flowers and birds in Fiji. The best places for bird-watching are Taveuni and Kadavu islands.

of plants have been identified, one-third of them native to Fiji. The most famous is the fuschia-like *tagimaucia*, which grows on the high slopes of Taveuni. It has white petals and bright branches. The national flower of Fiji is the hibiscus. Introduced from Africa, it is commonly used for decoration and food, and to make dyes and medicine.

Other edible plants include food staples such as cassava, taro, and breadfruit.

TAGIMAUCIA

The *tagimaucia* (*Medinilla waterhouse*) is one of Fiji's most beautiful wild flowers. Blooming in long, 12-inch (30-cm) bunches from late September to late December, the red flowers sport a small white center. They blossom on a thick green vine supporting large green leaves. The plant grows only on the banks of Lake Tagimaucia, in the high mountains of Taveuni, and all attempts at transplanting it have been unsuccessful. One of the most interesting features of the *tagimaucia* is that it comes with a beautiful and moving legend.

A woman and her young daughter lived on a hill in Taveuni. One day, the little girl was playing when she should have been helping her mother do the housework. Despite her mother's repeated requests, she kept on playing. At last, the angry mother hit her with the broom and ordered her to go away and never to come back. The upset little girl ran away crying. With tears rolling down her cheeks, she ran into the forest, not knowing where she was going. Blinded by her tears, she stumbled into a climbing plant hanging from a tree and became entangled in the vines. Unable to break free, she sobbed bitterly. As the tears fell, they changed into tears of blood. When the tears touched the stem of the vine, they were transformed into beautiful, blood-red flowers.

Finally the girl stopped crying and managed to set herself free. She ran back home to find that her mother had forgiven her, and they lived together happily ever after. Since then, lovely red flowers have bloomed on the *tagimaucia* vine.

FAUNA

Fiji does not have much indigenous wildlife. Most species were introduced by the first settlers about 3,500 years ago. One of the more interesting animals is the mongoose, a ferret-like animal that preys on rodents. Of the more than 60 species of birds, 23 are native to Fiji. The Orange Dove, which has never been photographed, can only be seen on Taveuni. There are also six species of bats and a few remarkable lizards. The crested iguana is one of the rarest reptiles in Fiji. Discovered only 20 years ago on a tiny island off Vanua Levu, it is believed to have drifted from South America to Fiji. Some snakes are also found in the Fijian archipaelego. One of them, the banded sea krait, is three times more venomous than the Indian cobra. Marine life is varied and includes most species of tropical fish. The leatherback turtle, which can grow up to 7 feet (2 m), is a wholly protected species.

The crested iguana.

THE NEW AND OLD CAPITALS

Suva became the capital of Fiji in 1882, thanks to its wide harbor and fertile land. It is now the country's administrative and political center and major port. In one century, Suva has grown from 200 inhabitants to more than 70,000. The town is continually expanding, and much of today's waterfront stands on reclaimed land. Suva is a cosmopolitan city, with many churches, temples, mosques, and cultural centers. The University of the South Pacific and the fascinating Fiji Museum are located here.

Levuka, the first colonial capital of Fiji, teems with history and old world charm. Sandalwood traders settled here in 1806, making Levuka the first European settlement in Fiji. The town prospered throughout the 19th century as sailors, whalers, and planters arrived. Before the capital was moved to Suva, Levuka was a wild and lawless place. Today Levuka is home to many historical landmarks, including the Cession site. Marked by a stone, this is where the deed granting Fiji to Britain was signed in 1874. The people of Levuka are mostly of mixed Fijian and European descent.

The town of Suva and its suburbs are home to half the country's urban population. Suva is one of the South Pacific's largest and most sophisticated cities.

17

HISTORY

HUMAN SETTLEMENT IN FIJI started more than 3,500 years ago. The first settlers, led by the legendary Melanesian chief Lutunasobasoba, landed near Nadi after a great sea voyage. They probably came from Southeast Asia by way of Indonesia.

MELANESIANS AND POLYNESIANS

The Melanesians were initially fishermen living in the coastal areas. They are known as Lapita people, named for a style of pottery they used. Lapita pottery is characterized by intricate geometric designs impressed into the clay before firing and is generally associated with peoples who had well-developed skills in navigation and canoe building. These early Fijians also left behind a series of rock drawings on a limestone cliff face in Vatulele, a tiny island to the south of Viti Levu. The petroglyphs, drawn by various

Left: **Melanesians who lived in Fiji centuries ago.**

Opposite: **The remaining colonial-era buildings exhibit an architectural charm.**

These petroglyphs date back to about 1000 B.C.

artists over time, include stylized human figures, fighting cocks, and stenciled hands. Around 500 B.C. the Lapita people moved farther inland and turned to agriculture. This shift in occupation resulted in population growth and increased feudalism.

Around A.D. 1000 Polynesian peoples invaded Fiji from Tonga and Samoa, engaging the Melanesians in large-scale wars. The Melanesians retreated into fortified villages protected by massive ring-ditch fortifications. There they planted taro on an intensive scale, using a complex system of irrigation. All land was owned by the whole community. The various tribes, both Melanesian and Polynesian, were headed by hereditary chiefs, and the people lived in *mataqali* ("mah-tang-GAH-lee"), or extended family groups. The chief, whose everyday responsibility was to find solutions to problems, enjoyed absolute power over his subjects. He was considered to be a spiritual being and could not be touched by ordinary people, especially women, who were deemed to be unclean. Marriages between the tribes were a good way of making peace, but tribal warfare was still very common.

THE WHITE MAN

The first reported sighting of Fiji by Western navigators was in 1643 by Dutchman Abel Tasman on his way to Indonesia. His descriptions of the treacherous Fijian waters kept others away for the next 130 years. In 1774 Captain James Cook visited the archipelago, stopping at Vatoa in the Lau Group. In 1789 Captain William Bligh passed between Viti Levu and Vanua Levu after the mutiny on the British merchant ship *HMS Bounty*. Although he was hotly pursued by the hostile natives, he made detailed and accurate observations of the islands.

It was not until the early 19th century that Europeans began to show interest in Fiji. In 1804 a group of shipwrecked sailors discovered sandalwood on the southwest coast of Vanua Levu, and the forests of Fiji were quickly ravaged by the beachcombers, who were mainly from Australia. This scented wood was bought for $50 per cargo and sold to the Chinese for $20,000. Within 10 years all supplies were depleted. In the 1820s, bêche-de-mer, a type of sea cucumber, brought the traders back. By the 1830s Fiji was flooded by sailors from Australia, New Zealand, China, the United States, and Europe.

In return for processing bêche-de-mer for the foreigners, the Fijians gained access to tobacco, metal tools, clothes, and guns. The availability of modern weapons caused havoc among the warlike Fijians. The local population was also decimated by diseases brought in by the white men. A measles epidemic, introduced by Fijian chiefs returning from an official visit to Australia, reduced the Fijian population by half in a century.

After meeting some Fijians in Tonga, Captain James Cook described them as formidable warriors and fierce cannibals.

CANNIBALS!

By all accounts, the Fijian people were a savage and brutal lot. One of their most repulsive practices, reported by the early Europeans, was cannibalism. For many years the islands were called the "Cannibal Isles," and this reputation kept many Europeans away from Fijian waters.

Cannibalism was practiced from about 2,500 years ago to the late 19th century. Prisoners of war, women captured while fishing, and shipwrecked sailors were invariably eaten. The worst fate that could be dealt to a captured enemy was to eat him. Eating a person meant destroying their spirit. Dead bodies were usually consumed on the battlefield, but live prisoners were brought back to the village and sacrificed to the local war god before being cooked and eaten on the god's behalf. In some cases the victors' cruelty went so far as to throw the victims alive into the ovens, make them watch their body parts being eaten, or even forcing them to eat some themselves.

Ratu Udreudre, a 19th-century chief on Viti Levu, was reputed to have eaten 872 victims. To keep track, he would add one stone to a big pile for each person eaten. According to his son, he never shared any of his victims, keeping the human flesh in a box so as not to lose any.

Among the more famous cannibal stories is that of Reverend Baker. The Wesleyan Methodist missionary, whose task was to convert the people of Viti Levu, unfortunately offended the highlands people and was killed in July 1867. His flesh was shared among the neighboring villages and eaten. The only thing that was left was a shoe, which is now exhibited in the Fiji Museum.

TRIBAL WARS

By the end of the 18th century, Fiji was divided into half a dozen small kingdoms. Firearms and the help of white men, especially the Swedish adventurer Charles Savage, favored the rise of Bau as the most powerful tribe. Although Bau is a tiny island off the coast of Viti Levu, it dominated western Fiji by the 1850s. Its chief, Cakobau, led a confederation of tribes and proclaimed himself king of Fiji.

In 1858 Cakobau arranged for Fiji to become a protectorate of Great Britain when Fiji came under pressure from the American government to pay an unjust $44,000 indemnity. An American trader and con man had accidentally set fire to his own home and trading post in a spirited Fourth of July celebration. As he had leased the buildings from the Fijian government, he insisted that the government pay him damages. He was backed by his government as the United States was also looking for ways to exert some influence on Fiji.

As Cakobau realized that he was not up to the task of governing Fiji, he offered to cede the country to Great Britain in 1862. His offer was rejected, and the Fijian chiefs organized themselves into a confederation. This arrangement could not withstand the deep rivalry between Cakobau and his enemy Ma'afu, and the confederation fell apart in 1867. A Fijian government was finally established in 1871, and Cakobau was crowned king. Two years later the government failed, and Fiji descended into economic chaos. In 1874 a second offer of cession was made to Great Britain, and this time it was accepted.

The site of Cession Stone is the spot where the papers of cession were signed.

Levuka in 1874. Soon after Fiji became a British colony, the capital was moved from Levuka to Suva.

BRITISH COLONY

Fiji became a British colony on October 10, 1874. The first governor-general, Sir Arthur Gordon, felt responsible for the protection of the rights of the indigenous people and decreed that all communal land could not be sold. He also instituted an administration that retained the traditional chiefly system. As the Fijian economy was in tatters, the governor decided to cultivate sugarcane as a cash crop. The Fijian population was reluctant to work on the large plantations belonging to foreigners, so Gordon imported indentured labor from India. This decision shaped Fijian history and politics thereafter. Between 1879 and 1916 more than 60,000 Indians arrived in Fiji. The indentured laborers signed ten-year contracts that allowed them to lease small plots of land in the second half of their stay. Two-thirds did not return to India at the end of their contracts. As no land was available for them to buy, many went into small business. Although the Indians decided to remain in Fiji, they resented their lack of rights and thus felt less loyalty to the country, compared to the natives.

Fijian warriors performing a war dance.

THE WORLD WARS

As a British colony, Fiji sent about 700 European residents and 100 natives to fight in Europe in World War I. At the same time, a Fijian named Apolosi Ranawai started the Fiji Company, a movement aimed at stopping colonial exploitation by the whites. A commoner, Apolosi questioned the powers of the chiefly system, which made this exploitation possible. But after being accused of sedition, Apolosi was exiled.

Fijian soldiers distinguished themselves during World War II in the Solomon Islands. More than 8,000 indigenous Fijians fought alongside the Allies in the Pacific. Virtually no Indian signed up because their demands for the same wages as the Europeans were not met. For this reason, the Indian community was considered disloyal and unpatriotic. Fijian soldiers were so good at jungle warfare that they were never called "missing in action" if they could not be found. Instead, the phrase "not yet arrived" was used because it was clear that the missing soldiers would eventually turn up later.

After independence, many Indians set up their own businesses.

INDEPENDENCE

Although the right to vote was granted to white women and indigenous Fijians in 1963, the Indian community still faced discrimination. Having witnessed the successful fight for independence in other British colonies in Asia and Africa, Indians started to call for independence, as they viewed the British to be the cause of their second-class position. The Fijians were less enthusiastic. Nevertheless, Fiji attained independence on October 10, 1970, exactly 96 years after becoming a colony. By then the Indian and Fijian populations were about the same size. There were also a number of Chinese and other Pacific Islanders. The Fijian Constitution followed the British model of two houses: a senate composed of Fijian chiefs, and a house of representatives. Fiji also became a member of the British Commonwealth. Although the Indians did not get the full rights they demanded, they agreed to a system of communal voting.

The first post-independence elections were held in 1972, and Ratu Sir Kamisese Mara, a hereditary chief, became the first Fijian prime minister. His Alliance Party, composed of Fijians, Chinese, Europeans, and some Indians, stayed in power until 1987. Although Fiji was an independent nation, the sovereign was still the king or queen of England, represented in the country by a governor-general. The first Fijian governor-general, appointed in 1973, was Ratu George Cakobau, the great-grandson of the man who had ceded the country to Britain. Fijian politics then was still dominated by the chiefly clans.

THE 1987 COUPS

The 1987 elections were won by a coalition of Indian and Fijian parties that enjoyed strong support from the labor unions. Although 19 of the 28 coalition representatives were Indian, all cabinet positions of vital Fijian interest went to Fijians, and the new prime minister, Dr. Timoci Bavadra, was a Fijian. The new government immediately set about to turn Fiji into a truly multiracial and democratic country, disregarding racist institutions and reducing the power of the hereditary chiefs. Faced with the loss of their privileges and financial benefits, the chiefs convinced the Fijian population that the government was pro-Indian and would take away their land rights. Demonstrations and massive unrest marked the first month of the new government: Indians were attacked, and the government offices in Suva were fire-bombed.

On May 14, one month after the elections, Lieutenant Colonel Sitiveni Rabuka, a commoner, led a group of army officers into parliament and arrested the government leaders. He set up a new government consisting of old-timers from the Alliance Party and made the governor-general, Ratu Sir Penaia Ganilau, head of state. Rabuka wanted new policies that would entrench Fijian domination in the constitution, and so Ratu Ganilau tried to work out a compromise solution to maintain civilian rule until the next elections.

As Rabuka was not satisfied with the way things were turning out, he staged a second coup in September 1987. This time he declared Fiji a republic and proclaimed himself head of state. His new council of ministers was made up of powerful landowners and military officers. In October Fiji was expelled from the Commonwealth. Ratu Mara came back as prime minister in December, and Ratu Ganilau became the first Fijian president. Rabuka himself was the minister of home affairs.

After the two coups, the Indian community—which included many rich businessmen—fled the country in droves, shattering the economy.

RABUKA

Sitiveni Ligamamada Rabuka was born September 13, 1948. He joined the army in 1968 and had attained the rank of lieutenant colonel when he launched his coups in 1987. Rabuka was a dedicated soldier who had served in various peacekeeping missions. An ambitious officer, he felt he was stagnating in the army.

A devout Christian, Rabuka is also extremely nationalistic. For him, Fiji belongs to the Fijians. His view of the Indian community is highly unfavorable: as Indians are not Christians, they cannot be trusted. A lay preacher, Rabuka believes that Christianity is the foundation of Fijian society. If Indians were to convert to Christianity, he would welcome them with open arms. Although he is not a chief himself, Rabuka strongly believes in the chiefly system. He sees himself as a warrior for his chief. His job is to protect his clan and bring glory to his chief.

Many political observers have argued that Rabuka was a pawn in the hands of various

factions when he staged his coups. The most accepted version was that his coup was sponsored by the American Central Intelligence Agency. The coalition government of Dr. Bavadra had announced the banning of nuclear ships from Fiji, with special emphasis on a nuclear-free Pacific. This was not welcomed by the American government, which sees nuclear engagement in the Pacific as vital for its own defense. Before the first coup in May 1987, Rabuka held discussions with a former CIA deputy director, and this was seen as evidence of the involvement of the United States in the coup. Another theory saw the influence of the Methodist Church, which wanted Fiji to be run as a Christian fundamentalist state. Yet another version stated that Rabuka was used by the chiefs to regain their privileges.

Whatever reason led Rabuka to plot his coups in 1987, he is seen as his own man today. After leaving the army, where he had been promoted to the rank of major general, he carved out a respectable political career for himself. Rabuka is credited with having brought Fiji back from the brink of economic bankruptcy.

RETURN TO CIVILIAN GOVERNMENT

After promulgating a totally discriminatory constitution in 1990, Rabuka, who had given up his military career to concentrate on politics, was elected prime minister in the 1992 elections. To repair damages to the economy and regain international acceptance, Rabuka softened his stance after becoming prime minister and promised to review Fijian policies.

In 1994 parliament was dissolved, and a new general election was called. During the campaign, President Ratu Penaia Ganilau died, and the Great Council of Chiefs elected Ratu Mara in his place. Rabuka was re-appointed prime minister.

A new constitution came into effect in July 1998, restoring full rights to the Indians. The document also changed the name of the country from Sovereign Democratic Republic of Fiji to Republic of the Fiji Islands. All inhabitants are now known as Fiji Islanders, a title that was previously only granted to the indigenous population. The new constitution created a human rights commission and established an elected, 71-member lower house of parliament. As a result of the new constitution, Fiji was allowed back into the Commonwealth, and new elections were held in May 1999.

In the elections, Mahendra Chaudhry's Labor Party won an overwhelming number of seats, but in an attempt to appease Fijian nationalistic sentiments, the new prime minister nominated many Fijian ministers to his cabinet. This decision was also seen as a move to prevent a repetition of the tragic events of 1987.

Fiji's prime minister, Mahendra Chaudhry, signs a document at Government House in Suva on May 19, 1999, after he was sworn in by President Ratu Sir Kamisese Mara.

GOVERNMENT

BEFORE THE MAY 1987 COUPS, Fiji was a member of the Commonwealth and a parliamentary democracy, with the British monarch as head of state. After the coups, the Fijian government became a mix of an English-style parliamentary system and Fijian customary rule. The 1990 constitution barred non-Fijians from access to the highest offices in the land. It also gave more power to the traditional Fijian chiefs. Following international disapproval and to gain wider acceptance in the South Pacific, the Fijian government enacted a new constitution in 1997 that lifted racial barriers to political life. This new constitution, which ensures representation of all racial groups in the government, came into effect July 27, 1998. The first elections under this freer constitution took place in May 1999.

The Great Council of Chiefs is also known as the Bose Levu Vakaturaga *("BOH-say LAY-voo vah-KAH-too-RAH-gah").*

Opposite: **A guard stands vigilantly outside Government House.**

GREAT COUNCIL OF CHIEFS

Although Fiji has changed to a Western-style government, the hereditary chiefs still wield much influence and power over the destiny of the country. Consisting of 80 members, the Great Council of Chiefs includes members of the lower house of parliament as well as nominated chiefs from the provincial councils. In addition to advising the president on government appointments, the council also has authority over any legislation relating to land ownership and common rights. Council meetings are chaired by the Fijian Affairs minister.

In a strictly hereditary society like Fiji, the chiefs have never lost their power, despite nearly a century of British rule and three decades of independence. Most of the high offices in the Fijian government and judiciary are held by people from chiefly clans. The Fijian governors-general and presidents have all been hereditary chiefs. The title "Ratu," used by the present president, is one title conferred on traditional chiefs. One notable exception is Sitiveni Rabuka, who is not a chief himself but enjoys the strong support of the powerful eastern chiefly clans.

The capital of Fiji, Suva, belongs to the central administrative region.

REGIONAL GOVERNMENT

The Fijian archipelago is divided into four administrative divisions: northern (Vanua Levu, Taveuni, Rabi, and other islands to the north of the Koro Sea), eastern (the Lau Group, Lomaiviti Group, Kadavu, Ovalau, and other islands in the Koro Sea), central (the southeastern part of Viti Levu), and western (the rest of Viti Levu, the Yasawa Group, and other islands to the west of Viti Levu). Each division, except the eastern one, is headed by a commissioner, who is assisted by a number of district officers.

The four divisions are further divided into 14 provinces. The provinces are administered by a council headed by a high chief. Provinces are broken up into districts, which consist of a number of villages. The village head is a chief appointed by the village elders.

The island of Rabi, with a population of Banabans, a Micronesian people, is governed by an island council elected every three years. The Polynesian island of Rotuma is also self-administered. Its council is headed by a district officer, seven chiefs, and seven elected village representatives.

THE FIJIAN PARLIAMENT

According to the new constitution, the Fijian Parliament consists of two houses: the Senate, or upper house, and the House of Representatives, or lower house. Of the 32 seats in the Senate, 14 are appointed by the president on the advice of the Great Council of Chiefs, nine on the prime minister's advice, eight on the opposition leader's advice, and one on the Council of Rotuma's advice.

The House of Representatives consists of 71 members elected for a period of five years. To make sure that all communities are represented, 23 seats are reserved for indigenous Fijians, 19 for Indians, one for Rotumans, and three for general electors. The rest are open seats.

The Parliament Building in Suva.

Government House, built in 1928, is a replica of the Government House in Colombo, Sri Lanka.

THE LEGISLATIVE STRUCTURE

The head of state of the Republic of the Fiji Islands is the president. Appointed by the Council of Chiefs in consultation with the prime minister, the president is also the commander-in-chief of the military forces. The Fijian president serves for a period of five years, after which he can be reappointed for another five years. The maximum period of appointment is ten years. The current Fijian president is Ratu Sir Kamisese Mara, who was first appointed in 1994.

The prime minister is in charge of the government. He is chosen by the president from among the elected representatives as the best person to lead the country, regardless of racial background. This usually means the leader of the party holding the largest number of seats in parliament.

The prime minister decides on a cabinet of ministers to help him in his task of governing the country. This cabinet must include members of the various parties in the House of Representatives. Apart from the prime minister, there are 17 cabinet ministers and four assistant ministers.

NATIONAL DEFENSE

The Republic of Fiji Military Forces (RFMF) are responsible for the defense of the whole archipelago and the surveillance of the country's territorial waters. The RFMF has about 4,000 well-trained personnel, who also take part in building projects and are trained in basic trades. The RFMF regularly sends contingents to UN peacekeeping missions worldwide, and Fijian soldiers sometimes have the opportunity to train with officers from Australia, New Zealand, and Great Britain through several agreements between the countries. Fijian soldiers are excellent at jungle warfare.

The RFMF Naval Squadron, formed in 1975, maintains Fiji's sovereignty at sea. The archipelago has declared a 200-mile (320-mile) exclusive economic zone, and it is the responsibility of the Naval Squadron to conduct search and rescue operations in the area, and to ensure no foreign ships are exploiting the resources in Fiji's exclusive economic zone.

Above: **A policeman in uniform.**

Left: **A police station in Levuka.**

THE JUDICIARY

The judiciary is an independent branch of the Fijian government. It consists of a system of courts, including the High Court, the Court of Appeal, and the Supreme Court. The powerful Supreme Court has the final say in any legal argument.

The High Court includes the chief justice and about ten subordinate judges. It hears civil and criminal cases. The Court of Appeal consists of the chief justice, the subordinate judges of the High Court, and a number of other judges. The chief justice is also the president of the Court of Appeal. The Court of Appeal hears appeals from all judgements made by the High Court. The Supreme Court is made up of the chief justice, the members of the Court of Appeal, and other judges.

The chief justice is appointed by the president on the advice of the prime minister after consultation with the leader of the opposition. Other judges are appointed by the president on the recommendation of the Judicial Services Commission. All judges, including the chief justice, must step down when they reach the age of 70.

LAND RIGHTS

Aside from the 10% that was sold to Europeans and Australians prior to Fiji's cession to Great Britain, the majority of the land is owned by ethnic Fijians. Indigenous land is reserved for use by the 6,600 clans. Clans do not work the land communally. Rather it is divided into lots, with each family receiving one lot. The owners can use it for agriculture or lease it for 30 years. However this situation has led to dissatisfaction. Owners are extremely frustrated that their land is being worked by outsiders at low rents, while tenants feel that they are at the mercy of owners who might not renew their leases.

The Native Land Trust Board (NLTB) is responsible for protecting the rights and interests of native owners by reserving ample land for their needs and for providing suitable land for resettlement.

36

NATIONAL SYMBOLS

The background color of the Fijian flag is sky blue. In the top left-hand corner stands the Union Jack, the flag of Great Britain, to denote the relationship between Fiji and its former colonial ruler. To the center right of the flag is a shield. Running across the top of the shield is a yellow lion holding a cocoa pod. The lion represents Great Britain and the cocoa pod the natural resources of Fiji. Other symbols of Fijian agriculture are the three stalks of sugarcane, a coconut palm, and a bunch of bananas in three of the four sections of the crest. In the last, bottom left-hand section, lies a dove of peace, the main feature of the Fijian flag before the country was ceded to Great Britain. The shield itself is separated into four sections by the Cross of St. George. St. George is the patron saint of England.

The Fijian coat of arms consists of two Fijian warriors holding on to the shield that appears on the flag. A stylized canoe stands above the shield, and below it is the motto of the Fijian people: "Revaka na Kalou ka Doka na Tui." It means, "Fear God and Honor the Queen."

The Fijian flag has been in use since the day Fiji became an independent nation. The design of the flag was selected in a national competition to choose the country's symbol.

ECONOMY

THE FIJIAN ECONOMY has moved from a nearly total dependence on sugarcane during colonial times to a more diversified one in recent years. Although agriculture is still an important part of the economy, light industries are slowly contributing a larger portion of revenues. In the wake of the coups in 1987, Fiji experienced an 11% negative growth in Gross Domestic Product (GDP), the Fijian dollar was devalued by more than 25%, and inflation shot up to 12%.

Following strict guidelines laid down by the International Monetary Fund (IMF), the Fijian economy was able to recover within a decade. In 1996 economic growth was an encouraging 3.1%. Compared to the figures in 1995, foreign reserves increased dramatically by 15%, and total external debt fell by 4.8%. Today Fiji is looking forward to sustained good growth and better economic prospects.

Left: **Friendly Fijian workers giving resort guests a warm welcome.**

Opposite: **A Fijian railway worker takes a break from transporting sugarcane.**

AGRICULTURE

Agriculture is still one of the driving forces of the Fijian economy, although it has been overtaken by tourism as the main foreign exchange earner. The largest sector of the economy, agriculture employs about half of the total workforce and constitutes more than half of all exports. Crops are planted on the drier western sides of Viti Levu and Vanua Levu.

Sugar is the mainstay of Fijian agriculture, and the most profitable sector of the economy. It accounts for 40% of the sector's contribution to the GDP and about a third of all employment. Sugarcane is planted by about 23,000 farmers on small plots leased for a period of 30 years from the government or from Fijian *mataqalis*. Although most sugarcane planters are Indians, the Fijian presence is growing in the sector. After they have harvested the cane, farmers sell their crops to the Fiji Sugar Corporation (FSC), a government-owned company. A contract between the cultivators and the

Farmers preparing the land for crop cultivation.

A fresh-produce market located beside a railway station.

FSC sets out the prices of the sugarcane and also a quota for each farm. The FSC runs the mills that process the canes into sugar. There are three mills on Viti Levu and one on Vanua Levu. The sugar is exported via bulk sugar terminals situated at Lautoka (Viti Levu) and Malau (Vanua Levu). The Lautoka terminal has twice the capacity of the one at Malau. By-products of sugar include molasses, a dark syrup that remains after the sugar has solidified into crystals, rum, and other liquors. Most of Fiji's sugar production is exported to Australia, New Zealand, Great Britain, and the European Union through a number of trade conventions.

Other agricultural products include copra and coconut oil, rice, root crops, and vegetables. These are mainly grown for local consumption. One sector that the government actively supports is the production of timber. About one-sixth of the total land area of Fiji is forested, and the Ministry of Forestry has started a program of reforestation to supply the timber industry. Timber exports consist mainly of sawn logs, wood-chips, plywood, and veneer. However, there is a ban on the export of logs from indigenous trees.

INVESTMENT INCENTIVES

To set the economy back on its feet after the disastrous post-coup years, the Fijian government set up the Fiji Trade and Investment Board (FTIB) to find foreign partners for local firms or to encourage foreigners to set up companies in the country. The government favors partnerships with locals since less money leaves the country, but businesses that meet the government's criteria can be 100% foreign-owned if the investor does not want a partnership. Priority is also given to those businesses that are export oriented because they bring in much needed foreign exchange. Generous incentives include the repatriation of all profits, tax holidays, and the lifting of double taxation with certain countries.

Opportunities abound in the manufacturing sector, especially for labor-intensive industries that require a low level of skill. Garment and footwear factories, for example, employ a large number of people, women especially, and require them to have minimum training. Factories that export more than 95% of their output enjoy tax-free status. Incentives include exemption of customs duty on equipment and raw materials as well as a waiver of the licensing fees. Moreover, the business enjoys tax exemptions for a period of 13 years and a refund of the value-added tax.

Another sector where foreign money is actively sought is the tourism industry. Hotels import 80% of their purchases for food, linen, and glassware at concessional rates. They can also write off 55% of their setup costs against taxes over a period of six years. To encourage the development of a more upscale type of tourism, the government has implemented a new incentive package for five-star hotels. To qualify, the hotel must have a minimum of 200 rooms with an initial investment of $40 million. The company enjoys a 20-year tax holiday on all corporate taxes, reduced rates for electricity, and duty-free concessions on all imported building materials.

The Fijian government is also promoting the country as an ideal location for film shooting. Citing its breathtaking landscapes and modern amenities, it hopes to attract filmmakers from the United States and Asian countries. Exemptions on taxes and duties are some of the incentives.

TOURISM

The fastest growing sector of the Fijian economy, tourism accounts for 17% of GDP. It is the largest money-earner, employing an estimated 40,000 people. However, about 58% of total revenues are either repatriated by foreign investors or used to pay for tourism-related imports. Fiji is by far the most popular tourist destination in the South Pacific, attracting more than 300,000 visitors a year. Most tourists come from Australia, New Zealand, and the United States. The growth market for Fijian tourism seems to be Japan, which sends about 20,000 visitors a year. Japanese investment in this sector, worth half a billion dollars, includes two hotels in Nadi.

Most tourists stay in large beach resorts on the west coast of Viti Levu. They are attracted by the warm weather, excellent diving, and duty-free shopping. Most hotels are owned by foreigners and managed by European hoteliers. Front-line jobs go to Fijians, while Indians fill the technical positions. The Fijian Visitors' Bureau (FVB) is responsible for promoting tourism to the country.

One of the best hotels in Fiji, the Regent Hotel, offers many facilities for the tourist, such as a poolside bar and beautiful views of the sea.

MINING

The only mineral that is exploited on an industrial scale is gold. A small amount of silver is also produced. The only gold mine is at Vatukoula in northern Viti Levu. Employing about 1,000 men, the mine is owned by the Emperor Gold Mining Company. Production has increased in recent years with the updating of mining equipment.

Extensive low-grade copper deposits have been found at Namosi, to the northwest of Suva, on Viti Levu. The project to develop the site was put on hold in mid-1995 after disagreement with the Fijian government over taxation issues. The project would have turned Namosi into one of the largest mines in the world, totally altering the landscape of Viti Levu.

Right: **Gold was first discovered in 1929 on Vanua Levu, and it spawned a mini gold rush that lasted into the mid-1930s.**

Opposite: **Fishermen returning with their catch after a hard day of work.**

FISHING

The fisheries sector is one of the success stories of the Fijian economy and is the pride of the Fijian fishermen. Canned fish is the country's fourth largest export, after sugar, garments, and gold. Most of the exported canned fish is tuna, but mackerel is also canned for the local market. Fiji exports around 15,000 tons of canned tuna to Great Britain and Canada and a large amount of chilled yellowfin tuna to Hawaii and Japan to be consumed as sashimi (raw fish). Other export products are trochus shell, shark's fins, and bêche-de-mer.

Fiji possesses a fleet of 17 longline vessels, with 20 additional Taiwanese ships under contract with Pacific Fishing Company (PAFCO), a government-owned company dealing with fishing. PAFCO runs a major fish processing plant at Levuka. One of the most active plants in the Pacific, it consistently and very efficiently produces high-quality fish for export and local consumption.

The local market is supplied by local fishermen in small boats. Almost 2,000 boats are registered, manned by 4,500 crewmen. Nearly all the fishermen who supply fish on a large scale are men; women are only involved in subsistence fishing.

TRADE

Fiji is an important center for regional trading. Imports have exceeded exports by more than 50% for many years. In 1995 total exports amounted to $572 million, while imports totaled $864 million. Reexports— goods assembled in Fiji from imported raw materials, meant for export to other countries—were $104 million. These are mainly petroleum products sold to visiting aircraft, ships, and neighboring countries.

Fiji's main exports are raw sugar, garments, unrefined gold, and canned fish. Major imports include manufactured goods, machinery and transportation equipment, fuels, and food. Australia is the most important trading partner, supplying 32% of imports and absorbing 25% of exports.

A busy port in Fiji.

TRANSPORTATION

Infrastructure is quite adequate in the larger islands. There are about 3,000 miles (4,827 km) of roads, of which 375 miles (603 km) are all-weather roads. Public transportation, such as the bus service, covers most districts of the major islands, and taxis are readily available in the urban centers. Fares are fixed by the government. Many Fijians travel by "running cabs." This is a shared taxi, and the fare depends on the number of passengers. Another cheap method of transportation is the truck. Passengers share the back of a small, hooded truck for a rather bumpy ride.

The international airport is at Nadi. An airport at Nausori handles regional and domestic interisland flights. The national carrier is Air Pacific, which flies to various destinations in the Pacific, as well as Australia, New Zealand, Japan, and the United States. Domestic services are provided by Fiji Air, Sunflower Airlines, and Turtle Island Airways, which operates seaplanes. Aside from the air services, interisland travel is supplied by a number of ferries and smaller craft.

Many uninformed villagers still throw their waste into rivers, little knowing that their actions will lead to a severe depletion of marine life.

ENVIRONMENTAL ISSUES

The major environmental issue facing Fiji is how to dispose of waste materials in a responsible manner. Most villagers still dump their garbage anywhere, as if the trash were biodegradable. In the urban centers, only 60% of sewage goes into a sewer system. Factories and hotels also throw their waste materials, including toxic chemicals and dyes, into rivers and waterways. All these have led to a serious degradation of the marine environment. Marine pollution in the area near Suva is so severe that the consumption of fish caught there poses a serious health hazard. Tourism-related activities, such as scuba diving, yachting, and water-skiing, have further contributed to the destruction of much marine life, especially the fragile reef systems.

On land, logging and bad agricultural practices have led to serious soil erosion and deforestation. The result is large areas of unproductive land, as the precious topsoil is washed away. The main culprits are landowners out to make a quick buck.

THE FIJI DOLLAR

The Fijian currency is the Fiji dollar. Its value is lower than that of the US dollar but almost on par with the Canadian and Australian currencies. Written as F$, the Fiji dollar was severely devalued following the coups in 1987. Although the devaluation caused great hardship for the local population, it also attracted many tourists as a result and helped the country to earn valuable foreign currency.

Above and below: **Fijian currency.**

Fiji dollars come in denominations of F$1, F$2, F$5, F$10, F$20, and F$50, while the coins are valued at F$1, 50 cents, 20 cents, 10 cents, five cents, two cents, and one cent. Although Fiji is now an independent republic, there are still traces of its colonial past in the Fijian currency: the portrait of Queen Elizabeth II of England still appears on one side of some bills.

FIJI ISLANDERS

FIJI HAS A POPULATION OF 802,611, according to estimates in July 1998. Approximately 75% live in the towns in Viti Levu, such as Nadi and Lautoka, and in the sugarcane growing regions of Ba and Rewa. Vanua Levu supports 18% of the population, and the remaining 7% is scattered over more than 100 islands.

All inhabitants of the Fijian archipelago are called Fiji Islanders. Fiji has the most multicultural population of all South Pacific countries. Native Fijians make up nearly half of the total population. The other large racial group is the Indian community, which accounts for 46% of the population. The rest is composed of Rotumans, Chinese, Europeans, and other Pacific Islanders, as well as those who are part-European and part-Chinese.

The larger towns on Viti Levu are quite cosmopolitan in their population makeup. The smaller islands and villages are almost entirely composed of native Fijians. Indians predominate in areas where sugarcane is grown.

Left: **A Fijian mother and her two children. Although they do not openly express it, Fijian parents deeply love their children.**

Opposite: **From a young age, Fijian children are taught to be hospitable and friendly to visitors.**

Fijian women in traditional wear.

FIJIANS

The indigenous Fijians are people of Melanesian ancestry. Like the natives of New Caledonia, Papua New Guinea, Vanuatu, and the Solomon Islands, Fijians are dark in color and have frizzy hair and Afro-Asian features. Fiji has also been a meeting place for Polynesians and Melanesians, and Fijians have adopted the Polynesian chiefly system and patrilineal descent, where property and titles are passed down from father to son. Fijians also display some Polynesian influence in their physical appearance, especially in the Lau islands, due to their proximity to Tonga. In general, Fijians are slightly less dark and are larger in stature than other Melanesians, especially Fijians living in the eastern islands. However, those in the interior and on the western side of Viti Levu, where contact with Polynesians has been less, are darker than their compatriots.

Fijians live in villages along the rivers or the coast. Led by an hereditary chief, these villages can have anywhere between 50 and 400 people. Indigenous Fijian villages are hard to find because they are always located far from the main roads. In western Viti Levu, villages are smaller and society less rigid. An outstanding commoner who displays great leadership qualities can be elevated to the rank of high chief.

Most Fijian families are self-sufficient, growing their own food and making their own clothes. Although each family works on its own plot of land, communal life is very important. Fishing, village maintenance work, and ceremonies are performed together as a group. Individuals are discouraged from rising above the rest of the community. Fijians who set up a business are often stifled by the demands of their relatives. It is normal for Fijians to claim favors from those who are better off in the clan. This custom is called *kerekere* ("kay-reh-KAY-ray").

Indigenous Fijian women and their children. From the late 1940s until the 1987 coups, indigenous Fijians were outnumbered by Fiji Indians.

Many of the public transportation companies in Fiji are owned and run by Indians.

INDIANS

Most Indians in Fiji are the descendants of the indentured laborers who were brought to work in the country's sugarcane fields by the British. The first Indians arrived in 1879 from the populous provinces of Bihar, Uttar Pradesh, and Bengal (today's Bangladesh). Coming mainly from south India, they tend to be dark-skinned, with straight black hair and black eyes. Although the system of indentured labor was abolished in 1919, Indians continued to migrate to Fiji until 1931. The later arrivals, mainly from northern Gujerat and Punjab, were wealthier. They came to set up trading businesses that catered to the large Indian community.

Most of the indentured laborers chose to remain in Fiji at the end of their contracts. In 1986 Indians made up 48% of the population compared to 46% Fijians. The coups of 1987 led to a mass exodus of Indians, and by 1991 there were only 340,000 Indians compared to 368,000 Fijians. Many Indian intellectuals and much Indian money left Fiji for Australia and the United States.

THE INDENTURE SYSTEM

When the British took control of Fiji, they resorted to Indian indentured labor to work the sugarcane plantations they had set up. This system had worked well for them in Mauritius and Trinidad, and the governor-general had no doubt it was the answer to the labor situation in Fiji. Negotiations with the Indian government started in 1878, and the first 450 laborers arrived in 1879. They were contracted for an initial period of five years, after which they were free to go home at their own expense. If they renewed their contracts for another five years, their return passage would be paid for them. In the first five years, the indentured laborers had to work exclusively for their employers, cutting canes for 12 hours a day. During the term of the second contract, they were allowed to lease small plots of land or raise cattle.

Many Indians saw the system as a way to escape the famine and abject poverty of their home country. Others were tricked into signing up. The labor agents misrepresented the distance between Fiji and India and painted a rosy picture of life on the plantations, with promises of wealth and great prospects. They also did not explain the penalties for breaking the contract. It was only when they arrived on the plantations that they discovered the reality. The laborers had to cut canes for 12 hours a day, and sometimes even longer, with only a very short break for meals. Food was strictly rationed, and wages were low. If the laborer failed to complete the daily task, his pay was cut, and he was physically punished. Moreover living conditions were terrible; the workers had to put up with over-crowding and no leisure. In essence the system was no better than slavery.

Despite the inhuman conditions, two-thirds of the laborers opted to stay in the country after their contract had expired. For many of the lower-caste Indians, life in Fiji offered better prospects than in India, and many sent for their families. Between 1879 and 1916, about 2,000 Indians were transported to the archipelago each year, bringing the total to 60,537. When the system was abolished, there were about 40,000 Indians in Fiji.

In 1912 a Gujerati lawyer, Manilal Doctor, was sent by Mahatma Gandhi to look into the fate of Indian laborers in the British colonies. He arrived in Fiji after having witnessed the deplorable conditions under which Indians toiled in Mauritius. Calling for an end to this inhuman system, he organized strikes and industrial action. For this, Manilal was deported from Fiji. Recruitment of indentured labor stopped in 1916, and the system was finally abolished in January 1919.

Under the indenture system only 40 women were allowed for every 100 men. But in reality even fewer were actually brought in. This led to women being raped and traded like cattle. Girls were forced into marriage and became mothers at a young age. Adultery was rampant, and remarriage became a widespread phenomenon.

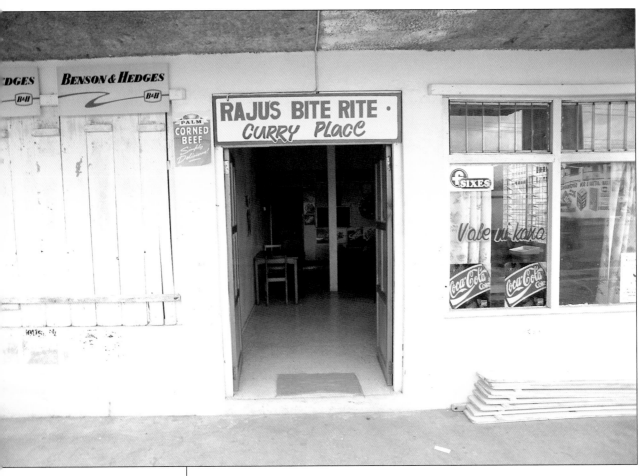

An Indian curry restaurant.

As they were not allowed to own land, many Indians invested their savings in businesses. Most village shops are owned by Indian shopkeepers, who are very active in the retail sector. Because their businesses are small scale, the Indians do not really control the economy of the country.

Although most of them have been in Fiji for four generations, the Indians have retained their ancestral beliefs and religions. Most marriages still take place within the same caste, although people from different castes interact freely in daily activities.

The Indian community is divided between Hindus (80%) and Muslims (20%). The Sikhs and Gujeratis, who did not belong to the indenture system, are considered an elite. In general, Indians still associate more closely with other members of the same province or dialect.

ROTUMANS

Situated about 289 miles (465 km) north of Fiji, Rotuma became part of Fiji when the island was ceded to Great Britain following wars between different factions on the island. The British decided that Rotuma was to be administered as part of the colony of Fiji, with a resident commissioner.

Rotumans form a distinct minority in Fiji because they are Polynesian. Although they have been associated with Fiji for more than a century, they have kept their Polynesian culture and language. Rotumans are a gentle people who do not practice social class distinctions, although there are chiefs. Social life is based on kinship relationships and communal sharing.

The Rotuman population is fast growing, increasingly made up of children and youths. On Rotuma itself, however, the number of working-age people is very low, and the elderly predominate. The Rotuman community in the urban centers is well educated. Most of the males are employed in skilled occupations or the professions, while an equal number of women are divided between working and homemaking.

Rotumans in earlier centuries. Of the 8,600 Rotumans in the 1986 census, more than 6,000 did not live on their home island of Rotuma but elsewhere in Fiji, particularly in Suva. Another 1,000 lived in Australia, New Zealand, and the United States.

BANABANS

"A Fijian father, married to a European lady, of course their children qualify as Fijian. A Fijian mother, married to a Chinese or European or whatever, their children don't qualify as Fijian, if they are married. If they're not married, yes," said Stan Ritova, whose Fijian mother and part-American father are not married, so he qualifies to be a Fijian.

Originally from Banaba (Ocean Island) in Kiribati, the Banabans were resettled on Rabi off the coast of Vanua Levu in 1942. This shift occurred after their island was stripped bare by phosphate mining and when the Japanese forces invaded it during World War II. The island of Rabi was purchased from royalties paid to the Banaban population by the mining companies. In the 1970s the Banabans sued the British government and the British Phosphate Commission for compensation. With the money they received, they set up various companies and even built a new house for every couple getting married on the island. Lack of business acumen, however, led to the failure of all those ventures, and today the Banaban population is as poor as when it arrived on Rabi.

The Banaban population on Rabi numbers about 4,500, most of whom work in agriculture or fishing. A Micronesian people, the Banabans originally did not take well to life in Fiji. Many died from diseases as their bodies, which were accustomed to the equatorial heat of Banaba, could not get used to the lower temperatures in Fiji. Originally ruled by a council of leaders, Rabi is today administered by the Fijian government through three administrators. The Banaban administrators have set up various training programs for women and young people so that the community can become more self-sufficient.

OTHERS

The rest of the Fijian population is made up of Chinese (5,000), Europeans (5,000), and part-Europeans (13,000).

The Chinese in Fiji are mainly descended from settlers who arrived to set up general stores or small businesses a century ago. Many originated from Southeast Asia, bringing with them their traditions. Today they are

still prominent in the business and retail sectors and are generally better accepted by the Fijians. Many of them are wealthy merchants who have worked hard and prospered over the years. They tend to work in restaurants and commerce. Although the Chinese have retained their language, customs, and religion, many have married freely with the other racial groups. Since the coups of 1987, the Chinese population has grown substantially, with about 1,000 mainland Chinese entering the country to operate market gardens.

The European community is composed of the descendants of Australians and New Zealanders who came to Fiji in the 19th century to set up cotton, copra, or sugarcane plantations. Many of them married Fijian women to create today's part-European community. All of them are urban dwellers, and most of them are well educated and better off than native Fijians and Indians.

Children from different races are taught to live harmoniously with their multiracial neighbors.

LIFESTYLE

FIJI HAS A LARGE URBANIZED POPULATION. Nearly two-fifths of the total population live in towns, especially Suva, which is becoming very crowded. Town life revolves around work or school during the week and church on weekends. Village life is more communal, with villagers coming together to share a drink or gossip in the evenings. Except in the towns, Fijians and Indians do not, as a rule, live together.

Nevertheless race relations are quite harmonious. Fijians and Indians do work together and interact on a social basis. Some may even call each other "brothers." Although one national identity has not developed, the two races live side by side with tolerance, while retaining their ancestral customs and traditions. Perhaps the one truly national activity is the drinking of *kava* ("KAH-vah"), a slightly intoxicating drink made from the dried roots of the pepper plant.

Left: **Workers unload food supplies from a boat.**

Opposite: **A Fijian man in traditional dress performing for tourists.**

BULA!

Despite their past reputation as cannibals and fierce warriors, the Fijian people are very friendly and courteous. *Bula* ("MBU-lah") is the most common form of greeting among the Fijians. More than a simple "hello," this word means "life." It is used to welcome guests, when meeting friends, or simply as a form of communication. Even though soft-spoken and rather reserved, Fijians greet each other with a smile and a cheerful "Bula!" or "Good morning." Except in the large towns, the same treatment is extended to strangers. Fijians today enjoy a reputation for good hospitality and warm friendliness, in stark contrast to the fear they aroused in visitors a century ago.

When a Fijian comes across an acquaintance, they always stop for a few words. Just saying "Bula" is not enough.

FIJIAN ETIQUETTE

Fijian society is highly structured, with many rules governing interaction. For harmony between neighbors, people talk softly and go about their daily activities with measured movements. Shouting or talking loudly is rude. Even children do not run around screaming their heads off.

Since Fijian villages are private property, all visitors, including those from town or other villages, have to seek the headman's permission before entering. They should be bareheaded, as only the chief is allowed to wear a hat. Many restrictions apply to a Fijian's head. It is considered the most sacred part of the body, so it is extremely disrespectful to touch a person's head. Even patting children's heads is almost taboo. In the old days, anyone touching a chief's head, even by accident, was put to death.

Another set of rules governs a person's feet. Anyone entering a Fijian house has to remove his or her shoes and leave them at the door. When entering a traditional *bure* ("MBOO-reh"), the person also has to stoop in a sign of respect to the owners and the people inside.

In the traditional village, men sit cross-legged, and women sit with their legs tucked to the side. Stretching one's legs in front while sitting is highly insulting, and sitting in the doorway is prohibited.

CUSTOMS AND TRADITIONS

Fijians have a great respect for the dead, so proper tombstones are nearly always erected for the deceased.

Fijians are very conservative and religious. However they have also retained many customs predating their conversion to Christianity. Some of the earlier practises, including tattooing and circumcision of young girls and boys, have thankfully been forgotten. But many traditional communal activities are still alive. Several relate to fishing.

On Lakeba Island in the Lau Group, the villagers perform an annual shark-calling ritual in October or November. About a month before the event, the spot on the reef where the calling will take place is marked off so that no one fishes or swims near it. On the designated day, the caller stands up to his neck in the water and starts chanting, which is believed to attract sharks. Popular belief boasts that during chanting, a school of sharks, led by a white shark, is lured to the spot. The villagers then move in to kill the sharks, except for the white one. The sharks are eaten later.

On another island, villagers catch a large type of mullet, a fish that is usually found in a freshwater lake. Once a year, clad in skirts made from

A Fijian presents a whale tooth to a visiting official. This generous custom of giving souvenirs to visitors is an age-old practice.

leaves, the participants jump into the lake and stir up the water. This activity causes the fish to leap into the air, and they are easily caught in the villagers' nets.

More commonly practiced throughout the islands is the fish drive. The whole village forms a large circle around the flat surface of a reef at rising tide. Holding a hoop made of vines and leaves, they slowly close the ring as the tide comes in, all the while singing, shouting, and beating the water with long poles. The fish are trapped in the circle and are easily driven toward a net near the shore.

One of the most solemn traditions is the presentation of the *tabua* ("TAM-bwah"). The *tabua* is a carefully polished and shaped whale tooth and is one of the most precious objects in Fiji. Once exchanged between chiefs as a sign of peace, today the *tabua* is presented as a sign of welcome or as a prelude to doing business. In villages they are used to arrange marriages, in sympathy at funerals, to ask for favors, or to settle disputes. Fijians believe that *tabua* are the homes of ancestor spirits and if buried with the dead, will protect them in their journey to the afterworld.

YAQONA CEREMONY

One of the most elaborate rituals in Fiji is the *yaqona* ("yang-GOH-nah") ceremony. It is performed with utmost gravity to mark births, marriages, deaths, official visits, or the installation of a new chief. Only traditional utensils are used: the *tanoa* ("TAH-nwah") is a large wooden bowl in which the drink is mixed, and the *bilo* ("MBIH-loh") is a cup made from half a coconut shell. A *yaqona* ceremony is full of ritual and pomp.

All participants sit in a circle on a large woven mat in front of the *tanoa*. A reddish-colored cord decorated with cowry shells hangs from the front of the bowl, and the guest of honor or most important chief sits near it. Stepping over the cord is not allowed. The *kava* mixer stands behind the *tanoa*, and next to him, the *kava* server. Women do not usually take part in the ceremony. When they do, they sit behind the men and are never offered the first drink unless they are the guest of honor.

To prepare *kava*, the *tanoa* is filled with water. Then the mixer places some *kava* in a cloth, dips the cloth in the water, and gently massages it. The water slowly turns opaque brown as the drink is mixed. When the mixer thinks it is done, he fills a *bilo* and passes it to the guest of honor to taste. If the latter finds it acceptable, the mixer runs his hands around the *tanoa*, claps three times, and proclaims, "The *kava* is ready, my chief."

Now the drinking proper starts. Squatting before the *tanoa*, the mixer fills a cup, passes it to the server, who gives it to the first participant. The drinker claps once to receive the drink and downs the whole cup in one gulp. Everybody then claps three times, and the cup is passed back to the server. The same ritual takes place again until every participant has had his drink. When the bowl is empty, the mixer announces, "The bowl is empty, my chief," runs his hands around it again, and claps three times. This signifies the end of the ceremony. A second bowl may be mixed and drunk, but with less ritual. The whole ceremony takes place in silence. However, after the first bowl, conversation is allowed.

EDUCATION

Fiji has a good education system, with a high literacy rate of 87%. Education is not compulsory, and most schools are run by local committees or religious groups. Thus Fijian schools tend to be of one race only, although the government has no policy of racial segregation in schools.

Almost all children attend elementary and secondary school. Elementary school lasts six years, and in the first four years, the medium of instruction is the student's mother tongue. Fijian children are taught in the Bauan dialect, the dominant dialect in the country. Indian children either learn in Hindi (for Hindus) or in Urdu (for Muslims). The Chinese community also runs its own schools, while European children are taught in English. The English language becomes the main medium of instruction for everyone in the fifth year of school.

Secondary school lasts six years. There are two major exams: the Fiji Junior Certificate in the fourth year and the Fiji School Leaving Certificate in the sixth year. Students can stay on for a seventh year and take the Fiji Seventh Form Exam. This is the equivalent of the foundation year in university.

Higher education is available at the University of the South Pacific. The USP is owned by 12 South Pacific countries, and there is another campus in western Samoa, where the School of Agriculture is located. The Suva campus offers courses in the humanities, sciences, and economics. The university has more than 2,500 students, who come from most South Pacific nations, except for Papua New Guinea and the French and

Schoolchildren waiting for classes to begin.

A public school in Levuka.

American territories. The Fiji School of Medicine trains doctors, while nurses receive their education at the Fiji School of Nursing. A theological college also offers courses in religious studies.

In addition, a number of technical and vocational institutions cater to those who wish to learn a trade or skill. Many of these institutions are run by religious authorities, but the government has increased its investment in technical education as it realizes its growing importance.

SOCIAL PROBLEMS

The main problem facing the Fijian people is that of change. With modern development comes a breakdown of communal living, and many young Fijians are looking for work in the large towns, in particular Suva. Without the traditional support of their village community, many live confused lives and end up causing social problems.

Migration from rural areas to urban centers has increased over the years, resulting in overcrowded conditions in towns. Unemployment, inadequate

housing and educational facilities, and a rise in crime, especially thefts, can mostly be attributed to urban migration. Suva faces a serious housing problem, with a rising squatter class. There are about 5,000 squatter families in Fiji, living in substandard and unstable structures that are easily destroyed by hurricanes and earthquakes. In Suva alone, more than 10,000 individuals have to put up with such living conditions, cramming into small houses without the basic amenities. Those living in housing estates provided by the Housing Authority of Fiji do not fare much better. Although they have a sound roof above their heads and proper sanitation, they face the usual problems associated with housing estates: crime, alcoholism, vandalism, and antisocial behavior.

Alcoholism and gambling are fast becoming major problems. With *kava* drinking entrenched in the lifestyle of most Fiji Islanders, alcoholism is one of the scourges that the churches are fighting to contain. Lotteries are very popular in Fiji, and it is even possible to place bets on Australian horse races at betting shops in the urban areas.

The rise in the crime rate is also the result of an increase in the number of school dropouts.

HEALTHCARE

Fiji's population is in generally good health, although the rise in diabetes, sexually-transmitted diseases, alcoholism, and malnutrition is worrisome. These diseases are all linked with growing economic affluence and a changing diet, and the health authorities are trying their best to educate the population about them. The government is also concentrating on improving environmental health, such as providing better sanitation and water supply.

Healthcare infrastructure in Fiji compares favorably with most Asian countries and even the lower-income Western European nations. There is one doctor for every 2,500 people and one nurse for every 500 people. Healthcare is provided by three national hospitals, 15 provincial hospitals, 54 health centers, and 96 nursing stations. In addition there are two government-subsidized private hospitals, three specialist hospitals, and about 100 doctors in private practice. Healthcare is not provided free but is generally inexpensive.

FIJIAN DRESS

The traditional Fijian garment for both men and women is the *sulu* ("SOO-loo"), a wraparound skirt. Traditionally made of *masi* ("MAH-sih") or bark cloth, *sulus* are now styled in industrial cotton. Men wear their *sulus* mid-calf while women wear them down to the ankles. Formal or ceremonial occasions call for more geometric patterns and muted colors. A short *sulu* is part of the Fijian military uniform. Grass skirts are worn during traditional ceremonies, such as *yaqona* ceremonies and dance performances for the tourists. The costumes are made of plain dyed grass and feature flowers as ornaments.

Indian women wear the *sari* ("SAHR-ree"), both in town and in rural areas. It consists of a short blouse called *choli* ("CHOH-lih") and a wraparound skirt with one end draped over the left shoulder. Muslim women and those of north Indian origin opt for a long-sleeved tunic over a pair of straight pants. Indian men rarely wear the traditional *dhoti* ("DOH-tih"), except during religious ceremonies.

Most men in Fiji wear the *bula* shirt. Resembling the Hawaiian aloha shirt, it is made of cotton and comes in a variety of cool colors. Floral patterns are most common, especially the hibiscus.

RELIGION

FIJI IS THE ONLY COUNTRY in the Pacific where religions of the West and East meet. The Fijian population has been Christian ever since the early missionaries managed to convert King Cakobau in the mid-19th century. As for the Indian half of the population, they have retained their ancestral Hindu religion. Christians make up 52.9% of the population of Fiji, Hindus form 38.1%, Muslims 7.8%, and the rest consists of Sikhs (0.7%) and others (0.1%). Only 0.4% of the population does not belong to any religion. Freedom of religion is guaranteed in the 1997 constitution and Fiji celebrates the main religions with public holidays.

The Fiji Islanders are a very religious people, whatever their denomination. Every village or settlement, however small, has at least one church or temple. Religious activities form an integral part of the lifestyle, and religious ceremonies are performed with utmost respect.

Left: **Fijian women today are treated with much more respect than their pre-Christianity sisters. In traditional Fijian religion, when a man died, his wife was strangled to accompany him to the afterlife.**

Opposite: **The colorful and elaborate Sri Siva Subramaniya Swami Temple is modeled after traditional South Indian Hindu temples.**

73

CHRISTIANITY

The largest religion in Fiji is Christianity. Almost all Fijians and 2% of Fiji Indians belong to a Christian denomination. The major denominations are Methodist and Roman Catholic. The Methodists are the most powerful among the Christian groups in Fiji. More than three-quarters of Fijians belong to this denomination. Smaller churches are the Anglicans, Presbyterians, and Seventh-Day Adventists. The Mormons and other evangelical sects are newer arrivals who use foreigners to disseminate their messages. With the Pacific Theological College and the Pacific Regional Seminary located in Suva, Fiji is a sort of Pacific Islands Bible Belt. The South Pacific is one of the few areas in the world where there is a surplus of ministers of religion.

The first missionaries from the London Missionary Society arrived in Fiji in the 1830s to find converts to Christianity and to preach against cannibalism. They did not have much success until they realized that they had to convert the chiefs first. The first successful conversion occurred in 1839 when a high chief adopted Christianity, together with all his villagers and the other minor chiefs under his influence. The turning point came in 1854 when chief

Cakobau realized that he had to become a Christian in order to secure the cooperation of the Christian king of Tonga. Many chiefs converted because they were impressed by the guns and machines of the Christian Europeans. Besides, the Christian concept of a supreme God was similar to the Fijians' own traditional belief in holiness. Many Fijians, however, continued to worship their own gods and ancestor spirits even after converting to Christianity.

Christianity is all pervasive in the Fijian's lifestyle. Christians attend church religiously, and their dress style is very conservative—their arms and legs are covered at all times. Most people dress up to go to church on Sunday, women in white dresses and hats, and men in plain, long-sleeved shirts and dark trousers. Church attendance is high, as all Sunday activities revolve around the church—church service, Bible studies, and other community activities. At least one church is built in a village or small town, and spiritual leaders are very influential and held in high esteem. Church singing is outstanding and filled with fervor.

Above: **Attending church on Sunday.**

Opposite: **One of the older cathedrals located in Suva.**

Hindus worship with offerings of fruit, flowers, and camphor. Chanting and the beating of drums are used to acclaim the deity. Fasting and abstaining from meat are other means to get closer to the deity.

HINDUISM

The indentured Indian laborers brought Hinduism to Fiji. Hindus generally keep their worship to themselves and have not converted any of the native Fijians. As those who came to work in Fiji were poor, lower-caste laborers, knowledge of Hindu philosophy is at best patchy among Fijian Hindus. In general, the wealthier Indians tend to be less religious.

Hindus believe in one supreme power, who takes on different forms and names in order to be understood. He can be both life giving and destructive. The aim of the Hindu devotee is to appease the destructive manifestations while imploring favors from the life-giving ones. Hindus believe in reincarnation and that people will have to face the consequences of their past deeds. In order to break out of the cycle of reincarnations and attain Nirvana, they have to lead a moral life. Their main path to holiness is through religious asceticism. Most Hindu homes have a small shrine for family worship. Each Indian village has at least one temple, but there is no fixed day for worship.

FIRE WALKING

Hindus perform a fire-walking ritual as part of the process of religious cleansing. Generally practiced by Indians from southern India, this annual ritual takes place on a Sunday between May and September, to coincide with the full moon. For 10 days before the fire walking, participants remain isolated and eat only unspiced vegetarian meals. Rising early and going to sleep late, they spend their time praying and meditating. Thoroughly cleansed at the end of 10 days and with their faces smeared with yellow turmeric powder, they make their way to the sea or the nearest river for a bath. The priest chants some prayers and pierces their cheeks, tongues, and bodies with metal skewers. By now in a trance, the fire walkers dance back to the temple grounds where the fire walking takes place.

Prior to the ceremony, a pit has been prepared with charred wood raked over glowing coals. Following the rhythm of chanting and frenetic drumming, each participant walks five times over the burning pit while being whipped by helpers. They feel no pain, and the soles of their feet do not get burned. Fire walking is the ultimate triumph of mind over body.

Native Fijians also have a fire-walking ceremony that is performed only by members of the Sawau tribe on Beqa Island, just off the south coast of Viti Levu. According to legend, a warrior was bestowed the ability to walk on fire by a spirit god that he caught and freed when fishing. Today his descendants act as high priests during the ceremony. Just like the Hindus, Fijians taking part in fire walking also have to abstain from sex and coconut for two weeks prior to the ceremony so as to purify themselves. However they walk on heated stones instead of hot embers. Only men can perform this native Fijian ceremony, while the Hindu fire walking is also performed by women.

The fire-walking pit is circular, with a diameter of 12 feet (4 m), and the stones are heated until they are white hot. The fire walkers psyche themselves up in a nearby hut. Accompanied by much chanting, they come out and walk briskly around the pit once. After all the men have had their turn, leaves and grass are thrown onto the stones, and all the walkers jump back inside the steaming pit while singing a farewell song.

Today fire walking in Fiji is mostly performed for tourists in resort hotels. The Fijian fire walking has lost all its spiritual significance and is not performed on Beqa Island anymore. As for the Hindu fire walking, many tour operators organize trips for tourists to watch it.

FIJIAN FAITHS

Prior to the arrival of the Christian missionaries, Fijians believed in a set of gods and spirits that had to be appeased and thanked. Most spirits tended to be malevolent, and they had to be kept happy so that they would not vent their wrath on the people. Fijians also performed ancestor worship, and the souls of outstanding ancestors were turned into local deities. A war hero could become a god of war, while a successful farmer could become the god of plenty.

Chiefs and high priests were worshiped as representatives of the gods. Priests also served as the gods' mouthpieces. Idolatry took the form of relics and carved whale teeth. The people offered food and *kava* roots for important rituals. Some of the more barbaric practices included human sacrifice and mutilation.

Fijians today no longer practice their ancient faiths. But despite being Christian for more than a century, traces of ancestor and spirit worship can still be found in their attitudes. The hereditary chiefs are still viewed as some sort of supernatural beings, although the Fijians have been taught that all people are the same. The singing and rituals in church are another example of the fusion of traditional faiths with Christian practices.

OTHER RELIGIONS

The descendants of Indian immigrants, particularly the Gujerati traders, Muslims believe in one God and follow the religious teachings of the Prophet Mohammed as set down in the *Koran* ("KOH-run"), the Muslim holy book. They are a conservative community who lead a strict lifestyle,

A tribal chief addressing his people. Although chiefs do not head traditional rites anymore, during special occasions, they are still called upon to speak to their people.

with many dietary restrictions. One of these is a ban on the consumption of alcohol. Young Muslims in Fiji are more liberal, however, and some even enjoy a drink of *kava* from time to time.

Sikhs also came from northern India. Believing in a combination of Hinduism and Islam, Sikh men are highly noticeable with their unshaved facial hair and turbans.

Buddhists are mainly Chinese. Worshipping Buddha, Buddhists believe in enlightenment, a state of immortality that will put an end to all suffering. The Buddhists have a temple in Suva and run a few educational institutions for Chinese children.

Although Muslims are only a small fraction of the population, at least one small mosque can be found in every settlement.

LANGUAGE

ALTHOUGH ENGLISH IS ONE of the official languages of Fiji, it is not the mother tongue of most Fiji Islanders. Almost everybody in Fiji is bilingual, or even trilingual. At home Fijians speak the Fijian language, and Indians speak Hindi. However they all learn English at school. All Fiji Islanders have at least a working knowledge of English since all official matters are conducted in English.

FIJIAN

The Fijian language belongs to the enormous Austronesian language family that spans half the globe. Fijian counts more speakers than any other indigenous language in the Pacific. Many languages in Polynesia— Tongan, Samoan, Hawaiian, and Tahitian—are derived from Fijian. However Fijian spelling differs from the languages of its neighbors.

Languages from as far away as Madagascar off the east coast of Africa, Easter Island, and Taiwan all share the same roots as Fijian.

Left and Opposite: **While some young people have the opportunity to pursue higher studies, others have to give up their studies after completing their elementary education to help out in the fields.**

Out of more than 300 regional varieties spoken in Fiji, the Bauan dialect is regarded as the standard form of the language. In 1835 two Methodist missionaries, David Cargill and William Cross, devised a written form for the language, which until then, had only been in oral form. They selected the Bauan dialect to represent the country because of the political and military supremacy of the island of Bau at that time. When they published a dictionary and a grammar, and translated the Bible into this dialect, the dominance of Bauan was entrenched. This is the language used in conversation by Fijians from different areas, in schools, and on the radio.

When Fiji was a colony, the use of Fijian was discouraged by the authorities in favor of English, but the language reasserted itself after independence. In 1973 the government set up a project to come up with a truly standard form of Fijian by creating a monolingual Fijian dictionary, but the project has produced no results to date.

FIJIAN PRONUNCIATION

Fijian spelling is still based on the orthography created by Cargill and Cross. Some letters are pronounced in a different way from their English versions. Although consonants are always separated by a vowel, the actual pronunciation may involve two consonant sounds. Fijian has no pure "b," "c," or "d" sound as in English. Vowels, however, are quite straightforward. Similar to other Pacific languages, the five vowels are pronounced in the same way as in Romance languages (Spanish or Italian).

Vowels can be short or long. The longer form usually takes twice as long to say as the shorter vowel. The short forms are:

"a" as in "father"
"e" as in "bet"
"i" as in "machine"
"o" as in "occur"
"u" as in "zoo"

A long vowel can have a mark above it, called a macron—for example, "mamâ." To pronounce a word correctly, it is important to note the length of the vowel sound. For example, *mama* means "a ring," *mamā* means "chew it," and *māmā* means "light." The word *māmā* is pronounced twice as long as *mama*.

Consonants with peculiar pronunciations are:

"b" as "mb" in "member"
"c" as "th" in "father"
"d" as "nd" in "hand"
"g" as "ng" in "singer"
"j" as a slurred "ch"
"q" as "ng" in "finger"

The consonants "k," "p," and "t" are pronounced in the same way as English, although they are much softer, and "r" is always rolled. The letter "v" is pronounced with the lower lip against the upper lip, somewhere between a "v" and a "b."

Fijians always place the stress on the syllable before the last one. Some long words with four or five syllables also carry a secondary stress. Not as pronounced as the penultimate stress, the secondary stress usually falls on the first or second syllable.

The standard Fijian alphabet uses all the English letters, except "x."

HINDI

Hindi is the language spoken by all Indians in Fiji. Although Muslim immigrants used Urdu and South Indian immigrants spoke Tamil or Telegu, their descendants today all converse in Hindi. Muslims may have retained Urdu as their household language, but they have adopted Hindi for practical reasons.

The Hindi used in Fiji is actually not the pure form spoken in India. Rather it is a mixture of the various Indian dialects brought by the early immigrants. One of its main components is Bhojpuri, the dialect of Central India. Many English words, such as room, towel, and airport, have also made their way into Fijian Hindi. Some words have taken on slightly different meanings, however. The word "book," for example, also includes magazines and other forms of print. Understandably no Fijian word is found in Hindi vocabulary. Hindi script does not use the Roman alphabet but a set of symbols representing 42 different sounds. Indian children learn standard Hindi or Urdu in school, along with English.

ENGLISH

One of the legacies of the British colonial rule is English, one of the official languages of Fiji. Used mainly in written form rather than spoken, it is understood by almost everybody. All schools teach in English after the fourth grade. In a country with two main racial groups, English is a non-threatening and acceptable third language for all official matters. Fijians and Indians usually communicate with each other in English. Most forms of mass media are in English, since they reach out to both communities.

Although Fiji Islanders learn British English at school, the way they speak English is influenced by the language they use at home. The Fijian accent is melodious and rather singsong. After more than 100 years, the English language in Fiji has evolved slightly, with some words or phrases taking on different meanings. For example, the word "step" means to cut classes. When a Fijian says, "Good luck to you," it does not carry the good sentiments usually associated with the phrase. Instead it means, "Serves you right!"

English signboards like these are commonly found in the cities.

Young vendors sell news-papers in the streets.

NEWSPAPERS

Although freedom of expression is guaranteed in the Fijian constitution, press freedom has different meanings for the government and the media. The conservative section of the population and the government feel that Western-style media opinions would disrupt the Fijian cultural heritage and harmony. At the same time the government wants to use modern forms of communication to promote development and disseminate information. But Fijian journalists are not to be reined in, and the major publications have had several clashes with the authorities over their outspokenness.

The main newspaper in Fiji is the English-language *Fiji Times*. Founded in 1869, it now belongs to the Australian-owned Murdoch Group. The government-owned *Daily Post*, also in English, focuses on local news. The government also publishes the *Nai Volasiga* in Fijian. Another Fijian paper, the weekly *Nai Lalaki*, is published by the *Fiji Times*. The only Hindi newspaper is a weekly, *Shanti Dut*, also published by the *Fiji Times*.

RADIO AND TELEVISION

There are eight radio stations in Fiji, broadcasting in all three main languages spoken in the country. The government-sponsored Fiji Broadcasting Commission runs five of them, with BBC News on Radio 1. Radio 1 broadcasts in Fijian and English, Radio 2 in English and Hindi, Radio 3 and FM 104 in English, and 98 FM in Hindi. Running since 1990, FM 104 is a music station that is supposed to play 10% local content. The songs of local singers are frequently played by this station. News broadcasts on all government-owned stations are prepared by employees of the Ministry of Information.

The three private stations are the commercial FM 96, which offers 24-hour music, sports, and community information in English and Hindi, Radio Navratang in Hindi, and Radio Pacific, which is operated by students at the University of the South Pacific. As Radio Pacific is a student radio, it is not allowed to cover political and religious topics. Instead they broadcast music and radio documentaries from different Pacific countries. Beginning its broadcasting in May 1996, Radio Pacific also features some academic programs. The independent radio station FM 96 started off as Communications Fiji Limited in 1985.

Television came to Fiji only in 1991, when Television New Zealand broadcast a live telecast of World Cup rugby matches. The only broadcaster is Fiji One, which is owned by the government and TV New Zealand. The latter manages the station. Programs, mainly American sitcoms, are aired from 5 p.m. to 11 p.m. on weekdays, from noon to midnight on Saturdays, and from noon to 11 p.m. on Sundays. Local content is negligible, and a clause in the license forbids the station from broadcasting "anything offensive to the Great Council of Chiefs." Only the islands close to Viti Levu receive television coverage.

Since Fiji is composed of many far-flung islands, radio reception is quite patchy, or even nonexistent, in many parts of the archipelago.

ARTS

FIJIANS ARE A VERY ARTISTIC PEOPLE. Many villages have retained their traditional arts, although for some, the main purpose is to earn some tourist money. While traditional arts such as pottery and wood sculpture are still very much alive in the country, Fijians have also adopted new and more modern forms of artistic expression. Young artists are trying their hand at painting, experimenting with different styles. One of them is Debora Veli, who paints stylized and naive scenes of the forest and Fijian mythology. Appearing mainly on postcards, her pictures can be said to represent the Fijian spirit in painting.

Fashion design is another new form of art combining Fijian motifs and styles with modern technology. A popular motif used by contemporary fashion designers is the hibiscus. Other artists have taken up photography, modern dance, and jazz.

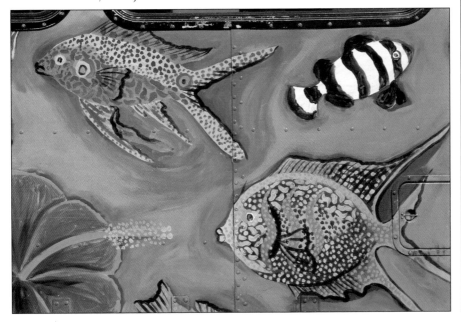

Above: **Interesting artistic details like these are commonly found in bures.**

Left: **Colorful artwork spotted on a local bus.**

Opposite: **A Fijian warrior in traditional dress practicing the use of his spear.**

Pottery in Fiji was mainly the work of women from seafaring villages, who traded their pots for food and other land products.

POTTERY

Fijian pottery is unique because most of the peoples in the region have forgotten how to make pots. Pottery making has been carried on by Fijian women for centuries, and different regions have different techniques and styles. Today's center of Fijian pottery is the Sigatoka Valley on Viti Levu.

The pottery methods Fijians use are known as coiling and paddling. The potter cuts out a flat round piece of clay for the bottom of the pot. Using slabs of clay or coils and strips, she builds up the sides. Then she knocks the pot into shape with a wooden paddle. A rounded stone inside the pot prevents the sides from caving in. The potter uses paddles of different sizes for different types of pots and for different areas of the same pot. When the potter is satisfied with the shape of the pot, she leaves it to dry indoors for a few days. When dry, the pot is taken outdoors and fired for an hour. To seal the pots, a type of resin is applied on the outside surface when it is still hot. While enhancing its watertight capacity, the resin also gives a reddish sheen that brings out the color of the clay.

LAPITA POTTERY

Lapita pottery is named after the Lapita people, the early inhabitants of the islands. Recovered from archeological digs throughout the Pacific, Lapita pottery gives us an idea of the length of time of human settlement in specific countries, as well as how the populations of the different islands are related to each other.

Lapita is an ornate style of pottery mainly used for ceremonial purposes. As Lapita pottery is very fragile, a large amount of pot shards have been found in many ancient village sites. The first discoveries were made in New Caledonia in the 1960s. Shards in this style have been unearthed on islands located in a wide arc of the southwestern Pacific, from Aitape on the Sepik coast of New Guinea and stretching all the way eastward to Fiji, Tonga, and Samoa.

The shards are identified by intricate geometric patterns impressed into the clay prior to firing. Some artifacts display patterns made of dot-like incisions, much like those used in tattooing. The finest example is a clay head recovered in New Ireland, east of Papua New Guinea. The pattern was made by a needle-fine, comb-like tool similar to those used by Polynesians in traditional tattooing. Lapita pottery has affinities with Asian pottery, evident in the shape of the jars, but the ornamental design is a local development.

The most valuable Lapita site in Fiji is the Sigatoka area, where sand dunes continue to reveal not just artifacts but also human bones. The most ancient shards date as far back as 1290 B.C. Other impressive pots found on Yanuca Island were made in 1030 B.C., while those unearthed at Vuda and Navuta date from 1000 B.C. to 100 B.C.

Lapita pots point to a sophisticated and highly involved social structure. About 500 B.C. the Fijian pottery style changed to a simpler form. Patterns were no longer elaborate, as simplicity and functionality became more important and valued than mere aestheticism. This switch coincided with a shift in population and occupations. Agriculture had increased significantly, and the population suddenly grew. People started to move inland, and cannibalism and the construction of defensive forts increased. Potters switched to a checkered decoration that lasted from 100 B.C. to A.D. 1000. It is believed that this sudden change was caused by a large influx of Melanesians. After A.D. 1250, the potters stopped decorating their pots altogether, and this plain-pottery phase lasted until the arrival of the Europeans.

The two most outstanding potters in Fiji today are Diana Tugea and Taraivini Wati. Tugea's pots are smooth and are used for cooking. Wati, on the other hand, makes pots for water storage. She decorates them with a raised pattern of triangular spikes, which are thought to represent a type of war fence.

WOODCARVING

Although most Fijians now use factory-made utensils and earthenware, the traditional *tanoa*, which is used for the daily drinking of *kava* in Fijian households, is still carved out of wood. Today it is the tourist industry that keeps Fijian woodcarving skills alive. Many items are carved for sale as souvenirs, including those that are no longer used by the Fijian people, such as cannibal forks or war spears, and even artifacts that were never part of Fijian culture, such as Polynesian tikis and masks.

The people of the Lau Group are the best woodcarvers in Fiji. Items for religious use are carved out of ironwood, which is considered sacred. Hibiscus wood is much lighter and more easily breakable. In the old days, it took years to carve a war club, as the carving was done in the living tree and left to grow into the desired shape. Today steel tools are employed. Shells are sometimes used to give a fine polish to the most exquisite pieces. In areas where the Polynesian influence is strong, carved objects are inlaid with shell, ivory, or bone.

There are many different types of woodcarving. For example, human and animal forms are generally used for religious objects, such as *yaqona* vessels.

LITERATURE

The Fijians have a long tradition of storytelling. Myths and legends are passed down from one generation to another in informal storytelling gatherings or around a bowl of *kava*. These stories narrate the origins of the Fijian people or explain the nature of plants and animals. One legend explains that the coconut has three "eyes" or indentations at the bottom in order to watch for people below the tree so that it does not fall on them. Traditional stories remain an oral tradition. Apart from some English translations, they have not been written down into books for Fijian children to read or study. Fortunately many Fijians still live in traditional villages, so this folklore is not in danger of being lost.

Fijian literature is mostly written in English. Although the literary community is very small, it is made up of talented and committed poets, playwrights, and writers. One of the foremost contemporary writers is Joseph Veramu, whose short story collection *The Black Messiah* has been well received in literary circles. His novel *Moving Through the Streets* offers a keen insight into the life of teenagers in Suva. Leading playwrights are Jo Nacola and Vilsoni Hereniko, who comes from Rotuma.

Indian writers express themselves in both Hindi and English. One central thread in their works is the recurring theme of injustice and the plight of indentured laborers. Prominent Indian writers are Subramani, Satendra Nandan, Raymond Pillai, and Prem Banfal, who writes from the perspective of a woman.

Above: **A traditional storyteller.**

Opposite: **A woodcarver adds the finishing touches to his work.**

SINGING

Today Fijian music is heavily influenced by Christian hymns, and more and more pop rhythms are finding their way into traditional performances.

Fijians are very musically talented, and they love to sing. Songs form a large part of the oral tradition of the people. In the villages local legends are told through songs. When the missionaries came to Fiji, they brought hymns and choir singing, which the natives readily embraced. Singing is a traditional activity, and the villagers felt a close affinity for Christian lyrics and music. Even the smallest village church boasts a choir, and Sunday service singing is fervent and of excellent quality. Church music includes both Western and traditional choices, and hymns are sung in both English and Fijian. In fact many songs have been written to traditional music. Although the title of Fiji's national anthem, *God Bless Fiji*, resembles the British *God Save the Queen*, the song took its music from an old Fijian melody. Most traditional instruments have disappeared, and the most popular musical instrument today is the guitar.

Contemporary singers have also been influenced by modern trends, such as reggae and jazz. Popular artistes perform in the major hotels and in nightclubs in Suva. Many have also recorded their music on cassette tapes, which are sold in music shops.

As for the Indian community, they are more attracted to songs in Hindi from "Bollywood," the Indian movie industry based in the south Indian town of Bombay. They like to listen to original recordings of movie music, usually a mixture of Western pop and Indian styles played with modern and traditional instruments. Local Indian singers have also taken to doing cover versions of popular songs. Indian bands perform Hindi songs at weddings and parties. Classical Indian music is less popular, although the cultural centers offer courses for the *tabla* ("TUB-blah"), an Indian drum played in pairs, and sitar, a long-necked, stringed instrument with a resonant sound.

MEKE

Meke ("MAY-keh") is a traditional performance combining song, dance, and theater. Reenacting legends and stories from Fijian history, *mekes* were held for entertainment but also to welcome visitors or to mark important occasions. Traditional *mekes* were handed down from one generation to the next, and new ones were composed for specific occasions. Before the missionaries arrived, *mekes* involved some spiritual possession, with participants dancing and chanting in a trance.

Men, women, and children take part in a *meke*, although the sexes have different dances. When they do dance together, such as in the *tralala* ("trah-LAH-lah"), which is a two-step shuffle, men and women dance side by side. Another dance with both sexes participating is the *vakamalolo* ("vah-KUH-mah-LOH-loh"), which is performed seated on the floor. Men usually perform war dances. Dressed in grass skirts and with their faces painted black by charcoal, the warriors form a line while brandishing clubs and spears. In the areas where Tongan influence is strong, paddles are also used as accessories. The women's dance is called *seasea* ("SEE-see"). Dressed in conservative *sulus* and blouses, or mission dresses, they dance and sing gracefully with their fans. All dancers wear flower necklaces, and women adorn themselves with flowers in their hair.

In a Fijian *meke*, the seating arrangement is very important, just as every movement and gesture during the performance has a special significance. Even the spectators have to follow certain rules. Important guests are given special positions in order to avoid offence.

ARCHITECTURE

The traditional Fijian house is the *bure*. It is usually rectangular in shape and is made of tightly woven bamboo walls with a thatched roof. In the past, tree fern trunks were used. In eastern Fiji, where Tongan and Samoan influence is strong, circular *bures* can also be found.

Bures are one-room dwellings with few windows and a low door. The packed-earth floor is covered with pandanus mats, and a curtain at one end separates the sleeping area from the living room. It is quite dark inside, and cooking is done in a separate, smaller *bure*. Except for numerous floor mats and some storage containers, the *bure* is bare of furniture. This is because its occupants sit and sleep on the floor.

Bure building is a traditional skill passed down from father to son. It is cheap and relatively easy and fast to build. When a family needs a new *bure*, the whole village participates in its construction. Since the house is made of plant materials, the walls and roofs require regular maintenance. But this does not mean the *bure* is a house that can be destroyed easily. It is usually sturdy enough to withstand hurricanes, a common occurrence in the islands of Fiji.

ARTS AND CRAFTS

Weaving is a craft that most village girls learn when young. In some tribes, only women can weave. The most common objects are mats, but baskets and hats are also made. Woven items make popular wedding or baptism presents and are also presented to chiefs as a form of tribute. The usual material is pandanus leaf, but coconut husks, banana stems, vine tendrils, and waterweeds are also used. The traditional method for blackening the leaves for contrasting patterns was to bury them in mud for days and then boil them with certain leaves. Today most weavers use chemical dyes.

Another traditional craft which is almost exclusively the domain of women is *masi*-making. *Masi* ("MAH-sih"), also called *tapa* ("TAH-PAH") in Polynesia, is the traditional bark cloth used in Fijian rituals. *Masi* feels like felt. When the cloth is ready, geometric patterns are applied with stencils made from green pandanus and banana leaves. Traditional dyes are rust, obtained from red clay, and black, made from an infusion of candlenut and mangrove bark. Plain *masi* is beige.

Above: **A Fijian woman making *masi*.**

Opposite: **Villagers building a *bure*.**

LEISURE

FIJI ISLANDERS, especially the indigenous Fijians, live at a relaxed pace, and leisure activities form an integral part of their lifestyle. Very few join in the frenzied race for material well-being. Most people prefer to enjoy their time in a relaxed manner, so long as they have enough to feed, clothe, and shelter their families. Because most leisure activities are simple and inexpensive, the Fijians do not have to work extremely hard to be able to afford the money for leisure.

In Fiji, Western forms of leisure blend with traditional, communal activities. Most men spend their free time practicing or watching a Western sport, but the most popular pastime is drinking *kava* with a group of friends. As for women, leisure revolves around church and other communal activities. Gossiping while working on a group project is probably the most common activity.

Left: **For many Fijian women, leisure means stopping for a chat with their friends at the market.**

Opposite: **Sailing is a favorite activity among the wealthier Fijians and tourists.**

Fijian men playing a friendly game of volleyball on a hot afternoon.

SPORTS

Fijians are very enthusiastic about sports, and they play all kinds of Western sports. Sports activities are banned on Sundays, which are reserved for going to church. Golf is an activity that has received a lot of financial investment, with world-class facilities in some resorts, but these resorts attract mainly wealthy tourists to the country. Not many Fijians are inclined to take up the game. Former prime minister Sitiveni Rabuka is an avid golfer though, and it has been rumored that many political moves, including the 1987 coups, were plotted on a golf course.

Another sport that locals and tourists love is scuba diving. With its wealth of coral reefs, Fiji is an important center for diving in the Pacific. Surfing has existed in Fiji for hundreds of years, and it is a popular activity with both locals and tourists. Windsurfing is also popular and can be practiced at more locations than surfing.

Rugby is the national pastime, and Fijians take great pride in the national team's achievements. A game similar to American football, it is played by teams of seven, 10, or 15. The aim is to score points by touching the ball down between the opponent's goal posts. Rugby players need to be strong and hardy since it is a sport with lots of physical contact. In Fiji rugby is played by Fijians only. The season lasts from April to September.

There is a difference in the games played in towns and in the countryside. Villagers prefer team games, and volleyball is very popular. Rural Indians like to play cricket. Lawn bowling, a sedate game that suits the Fijian relaxed attitude, is played by older people. Townsfolk like tennis and hockey. Soccer is enjoyed by everyone. Played by Fijians and Indians everywhere in the country, it commands a large following during the playing season, which lasts from February to November.

Having grown up in an environment that is surrounded by vast waters and beautiful corals, it is no wonder that snorkeling and scuba diving are the favorite water sports of Fijians.

RUGBY CHAMPIONS

The Fiji Sevens team were the champions of the Hong Kong Sevens Tournament in 1997, 1998, and 1999. The tournament is regarded as the World Cup of rugby sevens. When Fiji won the championship for the first time in 1997, the whole country rejoiced with a public holiday, and the government generously financed national celebrations. Following their win over New Zealand in April 1999, Fiji entered the new millennium as the undisputed sevens champion.

The national rugby team, the 15s, is also doing very well, having qualified for the World Cup in France in 1999. The victory was all the more sweet since Fiji defeated traditional rivals Tonga and Samoa to reach the finals. At the end of 1998, Fiji was ranked seventh in the world, and the country hopes to remain in the world's top eight at the end of the World Cup. At the 1999 World Cup, Fiji aims to finish second in its pool so that it can move on to the quarterfinals, consolidating its position in the top eight of international rugby.

As Fiji did not have a professional rugby league until 1998, most of the national players ply their trade elsewhere in the world, mainly in New Zealand and Australia.

DRINKING

Drinking *kava* is by far the most popular form of leisure for Fiji Islanders. Both Indians and native Fijians like to indulge in this pastime. *Kava* is not sold in bottles, as the drink has to be consumed as soon as it is prepared. Its elaborate preparation and the ritual surrounding its drinking is a way of building the community spirit. Sharing a bowl of *kava*, with the strumming of guitars in the background, participants immediately feel relaxed and close, and a bond naturally forms among them. Drinking is the Fijian's link with the past, the ceremony and ritual originating from ancient Fijian society. Today, however, Fijians regard it more as a social activity than a religious ceremony.

Fijians believe that drinking and singing go hand-in-hand. No celebration or gathering is complete without either one.

In the villages, men and women do not drink together. The custom is for men to gather around a large bowl of *kava* in a *bure* and talk while drinking. The women do the same, but they confine themselves to the kitchen. An old woman is allowed to join the men in their drinking sessions.

Kava is not an intoxicating liquor, so it does not make the drinkers drunk, and drinking sessions do not degenerate into drunken brawls. It is mildly narcotic, however, and the drinker usually feels reluctant to do any kind of work afterward. Its effects range from light-headedness to a mild feeling of euphoria. For this reason, government authorities view *kava* drinking as a social evil.

Although *kava* is consumed primarily as a social drink, local healers have used it to cure various ailments, such as tooth decay and respiratory diseases. *Kava* is also a diuretic, and pharmaceutical manufacturers use it in their preparations. Excessive drinking of *kava* causes a host of disorders, including loss of appetite, bloodshot eyes, lethargy, restlessness, stomach pains, and scaling of the skin. The latter condition is fairly common among heavy drinkers, who may consume up to two and one-half gallons (six liters) or more daily.

Because of the congenial nature of the drink, many business deals or contacts are made while drinking *kava*. There is always a bowl of *kava* in government offices for the staff to consume during their breaks. Visitors are also offered a *bilo*. Most people have their own *bilo*, which they keep in the office. In the old days, there used to be a bowl of *kava* in the back balcony of the parliament building for the legislators to share. Many police stations hold nightly *kava* drinking sessions when things are quiet. There are also stories of magistrates imbibing their favorite drink while hearing court cases.

Although beer and other types of liquor are available in Fiji, *kava* is the popular choice at social gatherings, parties, and religious ceremonies. Cultivation of the *kava* plant is a prosperous business for farmers all over the archipelago.

Drinking is also done at private clubs, a relic from colonial days. Although prominent signs proclaim, "Members Only," they are actually open to any well-dressed visitor. The drink of choice in the clubs is beer and other liquor, not *kava*.

Opposite: **A Fijian woman enjoying a bowl of *kava*.**

FUNDRAISERS

A favorite fundraising activity in villages is the drinking party. Organizers prepare a certain amount of drink, usually *kava*, and participants take turns to buy drinks for themselves and the others. To show their sincerity, they spend every single cent in their pocket. Those who cannot stand another round of the strong stuff can get out of drinking it by offering a reward for someone else to down the *kava*. Of course, the extra money goes into the funds being raised and not to the drinker. Aside from being a fun gathering, the drinking party also brings the community together in an activity that will benefit everybody. Many times school fees for the village children are raised this way.

FESTIVALS

ALTHOUGH FIJI IS A RATHER AUSTERE SOCIETY, Fiji Islanders know how to enjoy themselves throughout the year. Religious festivals of the larger Christian, Hindu, and Muslim groups are celebrated with a public holiday. Fijian festivals may not reach the carnival-like heights of other islands in the Pacific, but they are still highly colorful and allow the population to let their hair down. Hindu festivals, in particular, give rise to much public celebration and merry-making. Other secular holidays, such as New Year's Day, are celebrated with much gaiety throughout the Fiji Islands.

CHRISTMAS

The most important festival in the year for Christians is Christmas. For this pious group, the birth of Christ is the greatest cause for rejoicing, and most

Left: **A church choir celebrates Christmas with carols.**

Opposite: **A Fijian warrior poses for a picture before performing a *meke*.**

of them attend church on both Christmas Eve and Christmas Day. On Christmas Eve, church choirs sing beautiful carols, and the whole congregation joins in. Children, dressed in their best clothes, happily look forward to this day, when they receive presents of toys and books from Santa Claus. The Fijians' love of food is reflected in such festive celebrations. Much feasting takes place during these two days, with *kava* and traditional Fijian dishes being the highlight of every table. Villages throw huge communal parties, while people in towns attend smaller gatherings at friends' homes or in hotels. Many parties feature *lovo* ("LOH-voh"), which is food cooked in a traditional underground oven.

On Christmas Day and Boxing Day, which fall on December 25 and December 26 respectively, many Fijians go to the beach for picnics and parties. Besides an opportunity to unwind, this is also a time to think about the things they have done in the past year and prepare for the challenges ahead. It is also a good time for family and friends to get together. The festive mood continues to New Year's Day, which is celebrated by everyone in Fiji. In some villages celebrations last one week or even the whole month of January!

DIWALI

Diwali is the Hindu festival of lights. Literally meaning "a row of lights," Diwali celebrates the triumph of good over evil and light over darkness. Today Diwali is celebrated on a moonless night in October or November, one of the darkest nights in the year.

Weeks before the festival, Hindu families start to clean their homes and prepare little oil lamps. On the morning of Diwali, everyone puts on new clothes and distributes cakes and candies to neighbors and friends. Fruit and candies are also offered to the goddess of wealth and beauty. Hindus believe that the goddess comes to visit earth on Diwali night and that she will enter only the homes that have been thoroughly cleaned, following the light of the oil lamps. In the evening everyone gathers at the family shrine to say prayers and make offerings to the goddess. The children's foreheads are daubed with red powder, and the women draw good luck patterns outside the front door with colored powders. As night falls, the lamps are lit, and every Hindu homes takes on a fairy-tale appearance.

Muslims gather outside a mosque during the month of Ramadan. Many Muslims study the Koran more frequently and religiously during this time than at other times of the year.

ETHNIC FESTIVALS

Hindus celebrate Holi or the Festival of Colors in a big way. This festival marks the arrival of spring in India, and is celebrated in February or March in Fiji, at the same time as in India. Indian villages are awash with color as everyone has a good time throwing colored water or red powder on friends and neighbors. People dance in the streets, embrace each other, and exchange festive greetings.

Muslim festivals are much quieter, being a time to pray and strengthen relationships. Although only the birth of the Prophet Mohammed is a public holiday, Muslims also celebrate Eid al-Fitr and Eid al-Adha. The former marks the end of the Ramadan, the fasting month, and the latter commemorates the sacrifice of Abraham.

For the Chinese community, Chinese New Year is celebrated with lion dances and much merry-making. There is plenty of good food, and friends and relatives visit one another, dressed in new clothes.

THE MILLENNIUM IN FIJI

Fiji will be one of the first countries in the world to enter the 21st century. The 180° meridian, also called the International Date Line, crosses dry land over only two countries on earth, Fiji and Russia (Siberia). Three locations in Fiji sit on the date line—Udu Point on Vanua Levu, Mount Uluigalau on Taveuni, and Rabi Island.

Fijian tourism authorities are capitalizing on this event to bring in visitors who want to be the first people on earth to enter the third millennium. The Fiji Millennium Festival will include a series of events starting in 1999 and leading up to the year 2000. More events will continue into the year 2001.

Two permanent monuments have been erected to commemorate the millennium—the World Globe at Nadi International Airport and the Millennium Wall at Udu Point. The globe is a timepiece to count down the days to the year 2000. The continents are depicted in scenes showing the people of all nations living in peace and harmony. The Millennium Wall will be a major focus during the celebrations.

Before and during the festival, there will be many events involving young Fijians, in which they can develop a vision for the future of the country and consider ways to improve their daily lives.

One major event is the National Painting Competition to be held in schools across Fiji. The winning designs will be used on a series of First Day Cover stamps.

The millennium will also be the theme of the National Essay Competition. Fijian children will be asked to write about how the grand event will affect their lives. Four lucky winners will be selected to personally deliver the country's millennium message to the United Nations in New York.

Another major event is the National Song Competition, which will be open to entries from overseas. The World Festival of Praise is scheduled for December 26, 1999 to January 2, 2000. A nondenominational event, it will bring together religious leaders from all over the world to celebrate the festival in unity and prayer.

Other planned events include the hosting of the participants in the Millennium Round-the-World Yacht Race in March 2000, the hosting of the Olympic Flame in May 2000 on its way to Sydney in Australia for the Olympic Games, and the hosting of some 2,000 visitors from Japan in December 2000 to mark the dawn of the Japanese Millennium in 2001.

During Chinese New Year, parents and older folks will give each child a red packet, which contains a token sum of money, as a symbol of good luck.

HIBISCUS FESTIVAL

Started in 1956, the Suva Hibiscus Festival was based loosely on Hawaii's Aloha Week. The festival lasts over a week in August and brings together cultural performances by local and foreign groups, a glamorous beauty pageant, and a charity fund-raising drive. Every year the Lord Mayor of Suva declares the festival open, and a parade kicks off the festival, followed by a display of fireworks in Albert Park, which is located in central Suva.

Fashion shows, food tasting, music and dance, and games dominate the festival. The highlight, however, is the Miss Hibiscus pageant. Lasting over

The Hibiscus Festival is a much-loved occasion. Here the Fijians *(right)* **and the Polynesian dancers** *(opposite)* **are enjoying themselves tremendously with song and dance.**

two evenings, the aim of the pageant is to find the best ambassador for the city of Suva. Contestants are judged not just on their physical attributes, but also on their knowledge of current affairs and their familiarity with Suva. Miss Hibiscus is elected by public judging, so the judges mingle with the contestants, discussing various topics with them, in order to test their knowledge. A Miss Charity is also crowned to honor the contestant who has raised the largest amount of money for the Hibiscus Charity Chest. The proceeds collected from the charity drive are distributed to the needy in Fiji.

A daylong children's carnival caters for the younger segment of the population. Babies participate in a baby show, and prizes are awarded to the most adorable tots and their parents. Older children take part in an aerobics championship, and some of them participate in musical and dance performances, and fashion shows. It is a fun and lively carnival that many children look forward to.

Since Fiji is a largely Christian country, no event is complete without a religious component. The Hibiscus Festival features singing competitions between church choirs, and religious worship by youth organizations and church groups. These exciting competitions usually draw many participants.

FOOD

FIJIAN FOOD BRINGS TOGETHER all the various influences from the country's diversified population. Fijian, Indian, Polynesian, Chinese, and Western cuisines can all be found in the country. In the villages, the various ethnic groups usually keep to their traditional diets, but urban Fijians get to sample different types of foods. Suva and Nadi have all kinds of restaurants, catering to every taste and budget. Even American-style fast food has found its way to Fiji. No truly Fijian dish has evolved from the marriage of so many culinary traditions. Only Chinese curries combine two separate cuisines—Chinese and Indian.

In general, native Fijians and Indians use their hands to eat. The other communities use spoons and forks. Very few people eat Western-style, with a knife and fork. In the villages, meals are eaten on the floor, and the family sits on mats. When entertaining, Fiji Islanders believe that they

Left: **Two sisters sit down for a meal in their** *bure.*

Opposite: **The Suva market is one of the busiest markets in Fiji.**

115

should provide enough for their guests to eat their fill, thus the result is usually too much food. Some hosts even wait for their guests to finish eating before starting on their own meals.

Fijians, Chinese, and Europeans do not have any dietary restrictions, eating the meats and vegetables available in the markets. The Indian community, however, faces more restriction on what they are allowed to eat. Muslims do not eat pork and are not supposed to drink alcoholic beverages. However some young men do indulge in *kava* and beer. As for Hindus, they are not allowed to eat beef, but this restriction is observed only by the very conservative families. Some Hindus are vegetarians.

THE FIJIAN OVEN

The Fijian equivalent of the Hawaiian luau is called *lovo*. The whole village works together to prepare this feast. First a large pit is dug and lined with a stack of dry coconut husks. The husks are set on fire, and once the fire is going well, stones are heaped on top. When most of the husks have burned away, the food is wrapped in banana leaves and lowered into the pit. The fish and meat are the first to go in, then the vegetables are placed on top. Everything is then covered with banana leaves and more stones, and the food is left to cook. After about two and a half hours, when everything is cooked, the top leaves and stones can be removed.

A popular dish cooked in the *lovo* is *palusami* ("pah-loo-SAH-mih"). A mixture of chicken or corned beef with onions, tomatoes, and coconut cream, the *palusami* is wrapped in taro leaves before cooking. At times a whole pig is cooked in the pit. The animal is cleaned and stuffed with banana leaves and hot stones. This cooks the meat thoroughly.

Lovos are still prepared in the villages for special occasions, such as the inauguration of a new chief or a wedding, or for festivals, such as Christmas Day. However they are now more common in resort hotels, accompanied by a *meke* or fire-walking ceremony.

Opposite: **Fresh vegetables for sale at the market.**

Below: **A Fijian man prepares a fish for *lovo*.**

A Fijian man selling staples, such as rice and beans, which are essential ingredients in Fijian meals.

STAPLES

The most common staple food is rice, which is eaten by all the different racial groups. The country aims to be self-sufficient in rice by turning over large areas of sugarcane fields to rice cultivation, but more than a third of the total consumption is still imported. Indians also eat *roti* ("roh-TEE"), a flat tortilla-like pancake made of wheat flour and cooked on a griddle. As for the Fijians, a number of starchy roots and tubers go into their diet. Yams are considered a prestige food, but they are not as nutritious as taro or breadfruit. Taro is usually boiled, but breadfruit, which is an important food found everywhere in the South Pacific, can also be baked or roasted. When cooked, breadfruit resembles bread. Fijians also like to eat boiled sweet potatoes and cassava. *Vakalolo* ("vah-kah-LOH-loh") is a sweet pudding made with all the starchy roots that Fijians eat. Mashed taro, cassava, and breadfruit are combined with coconut milk and caramelized sugarcane juice to make this special delicacy, which is usually served only at traditional feasts.

For protein, Fijians consume large amounts of lagoon fish that they catch themselves. Fish is eaten raw in a salad or baked in coconut cream with taro and cassava. Beef and pork are occasionally fried and eaten with these roots. Chicken is called "bird meat" and is not so popular among Fijians. Exotic meats that are still consumed in Fiji include turtle and bat. Although turtle is an endangered species and is protected by law, turtle meat can still be found in the markets. Boiled bat, a foul-smelling and vile-tasting dish, used to be very popular in Fiji. Today, however, only the older generation favors it.

Indians prefer mutton or goat meat cooked in spicy curry. Muslims, on the other hand, cook their curries with beef. They also consume large amounts of yellow or red lentils. Cooked in soup and flavored with spices, lentils account for a good portion of their protein intake.

An Indian dessert that contains coconut. Coconut is used in both Fijian and Indian cooking.

Both Fijians and Indians have garden vegetables in their diet. Cabbage, beans, and eggplant are either stewed or cooked in curry. Fijians like taro leaves cooked in coconut cream.

Coconut is a very popular plant in Fiji. Its water is drunk as a refreshing beverage, while the meat is squeezed with water to produce cream or milk. An ecologically destructive dish is millionaire's salad, made from the heart of the coconut tree. To make one salad, a whole mature tree is felled.

The Fijian diet includes increasingly large amounts of canned foods. In many communities, the switch from fresh fruit and vegetables to the canned varieties is cause for growing concern. Canned beef or pilchards have been substituted for fresh meat in many traditional recipes. This reliance on canned foods is giving rise to many diseases that were not present in Fiji a few decades ago.

A shopkeeper selling *kava* roots at a market. Traditionally the drink was prepared by young women who chewed the root and blended it with their saliva, making the drink more potent. This unhygienic practice has died out.

DRINKS

Although *kava* is an integral part of Fiji's culture, drinking alcoholic beverages on the street is actually prohibited. Strict laws govern the sale of beer and liquor—for instance, alcohol cannot be sold on Sundays. The most popular drink, after *kava*, is Fiji Bitter beer, brewed in Suva and Lautoka. Local distilleries produce gin, brandy, rum, vodka, and whisky.

The drink of choice is *kava*. Made by diluting the pounded root of the pepper plant in water, it looks and tastes like muddy water. Fijians swear that hand-pounded *kava* tastes better than machine-ground root. But most of what is available on the market is made by machine and sold in small packets for instant mixing with a bowl of water.

Children and nondrinkers have a wide choice of nonalcoholic beverages. Coconut water is a favorite, while manufactured soda is consumed in large quantities. Although fresh fruit is readily available, freshly squeezed fruit juice is not popular. Fijians prefer to drink fruit cordial diluted with water.

KOKODA

4 large fillets of white fish
3 large limes
1 cup fresh coconut cream
1 large onion, minced
1 chili (or 1 teaspoon Tabasco sauce)
2 medium tomatoes, diced
1 large bell pepper, diced
salt to taste

Cut raw fish into bite-sized pieces. Marinate overnight in juice of limes. This process "cooks" the fish. Add coconut cream, chopped onion, and chili to taste just before serving. Decorate with diced tomatoes and bell pepper. Serve in a large bowl or on a bed of lettuce in coconut *bilos*.

Caution: The *kokoda* ("koh-KONG-dah") will solidify if it is refrigerated too long after the ingredients have been combined.

A two-storey building, the Suva municipal market also sells colorful handicrafts. It is one of the few places where all races in the country are represented.

MARKETS

Fijians buy their produce from a variety of sources. They can get a few vegetables from an Indian woman selling her garden produce in front of her house or visit the market or supermarket. All the towns have a municipal market as well as a well-stocked supermarket. Villagers are usually self-sufficient in fresh produce.

The Suva Municipal Market is the largest retail produce market in the Pacific. Polynesian, Chinese, Indian, and Fijian vendors sell fish, meat, vegetables, fruit, coconut oil, and nearly everything else that a Fijian household might need. The first level contains all the fresh meats and vegetables, while dried goods are found upstairs. Large areas are devoted to the sale of *kava,* whole and ground. The Indian spices section is a mix of aromas and colors. Indian sweets are sold from kiosks at one side of the market. Some of the confections are actually not sweet but spicy. There is also a *yaqona* saloon outdoors dedicated solely to *kava* drinkers. Passers-by are urged to try a bowl by energetic salesmen. Fijian women also sell fresh pineapple and guava juice from glass containers.

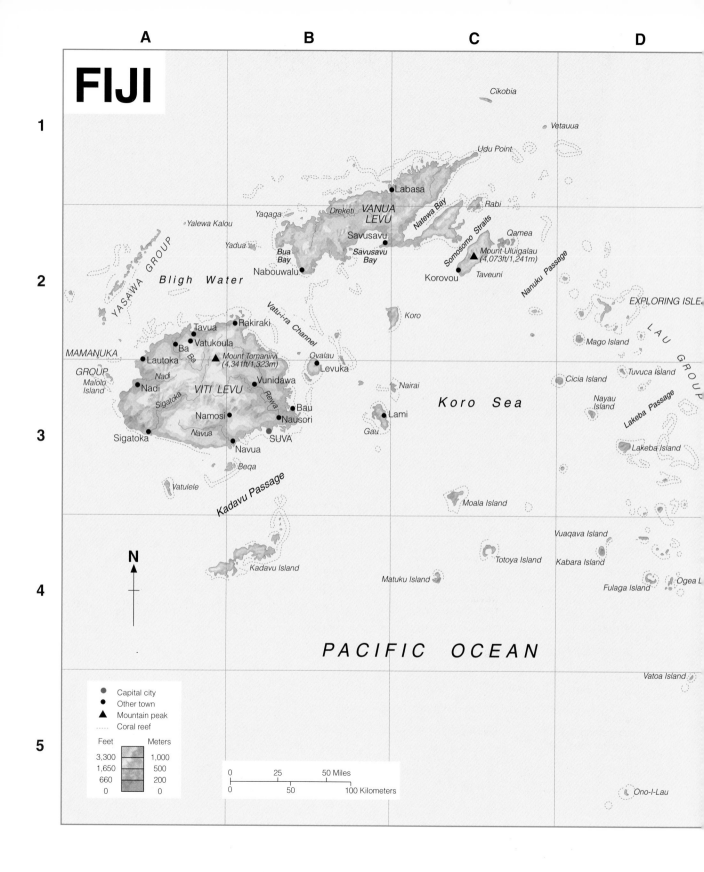

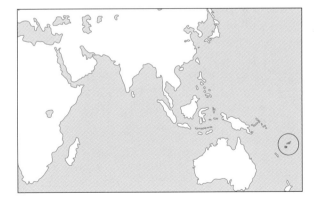

QUICK NOTES

Official Name
Republic of the Fiji Islands

National Anthem
God Bless Fiji

Official motto
Fear God and honor the Queen

National Flower
Hibiscus

National Drink
kava

Total Area
501,800 square miles (1,300,000 square km)

Population
802,611 people (July 1998 estimate)

Population Growth Rate
1.3% (July 1998 estimate)

Capital
Suva

Major Rivers
Rewa, Sigatoka, Ba

Climate
Tropical marine

Highest Point
Mount Tomaniivi (4,341 feet / 1,323 m)

Currency
Fiji dollar
F$1=100 cents (US$1=F$1.97)

Major Imports
Manufactured goods, machinery and transportation equipment, fuels, and food

Major Exports
Sugar, garments, unrefined gold, canned fish, coconut oil, timber, and ginger

Ethnic Groups
Fijian (49%), Indian (46%), European, other Pacific Islanders, Chinese

Major Languages
English, Fijian, Hindi

Literacy Rate
87%

Religions
Christians (52.9%), Hindus (38.1%), Muslims (7.8%), Sikhs (0.7%), and others (0.5%)

Famous Leaders
King Cakobau, Sir Arthur Gordon, Ratu Sir Kamisese Mara, Sitiveni Rabuka

GLOSSARY

bilo ("MBIH-loh")
A bowl made from half a coconut shell.

bula ("MBU-lah")
A common Fijian greeting, meaning "life."

bure ("MBOO-reh")
A traditional Fijian thatched house.

choli ("CHOH-lih")
A short blouse worn by Indian women with the sari.

dhoti ("DOH-tih")
A white loin cloth worn by Indian men.

kava ("KAH-vah")
A slightly intoxicating drink made from the dried roots of the pepper plant.

kerekere ("kay-reh-KAY-ray")
The Fijian custom of asking favors from relatives.

kokoda ("koh-KONG-dah")
A dish of raw fish marinated in lime juice.

lovo ("LOH-voh")
A feast cooked in an underground oven.

masi ("MAH-sih")
A traditional bark cloth with a smooth and felt-like finish.

mataqali ("mah-tang-GAH-lee")
An extended family group.

meke ("MAY-keh")
A traditional performance combining song, dance, and theater.

roti ("roh-TEE")
A flat tortilla-like pancake made of wheat flour and cooked on a griddle.

sari ("SAHR-ree")
A traditional dress of Indian women, worn as a wraparound skirt with one end draped over the left shoulder.

sulu ("SOO-loo")
A wraparound skirt worn by men and women.

tabua ("TAM-bwah")
A polished whale tooth used as diplomatic gifts in traditional society.

tanoa ("TAH-nwah")
A large wooden bowl for mixing *kava*.

vakalolo ("vah-kah-LOH-loh")
A sweet pudding of cassava, taro, and breadfruit.

yaqona ("yang-GOH-nah")
An elaborate ceremony for drinking *kava*.

BIBLIOGRAPHY

Subramani. *The Fantasy Eaters: Stories from Fiji.* Three Continents Press, 1988.

Dean, Eddie, and Stan Ritova. *Rabuka: No Other Way.* Sydney, Australia: Doubleday, 1988.

Ulack, Richard. *Fiji (Around the World Program Series),* McDonald & Woodward Pub. Co., 1995.

Wibberley, Leonard. *Fiji: Islands of the Dawn,* New York: Ives Washburn Inc., 1964.

INDEX

INDEX

INDEX

PICTURE CREDITS